CODE RED

A YOUNG CHRISTIAN SURGEON
FINDS *JOB* HELPS HIM FACE DEATH

ANDREW J DRAIN

For I consider that the sufferings of this present time are not worth comparing with the glory that is to be revealed to us.

(ROMANS 8:18)

CODE RED

Andrew J Drain
CODE RED
© 2010 The estate of Andrew J Drain
All rights reserved
Published by Christian Medical Fellowship
6 Marshalsea Road, London SE1 1HL, UK
www.cmf.org.uk

ISBN 978-0-906747-40-7

Printed by Stanley L. Hunt (Printers) *www.stanleylhunt.co.uk*
Cover design by S2 Design & Advertising
enquiries@s2design.co.uk

CONTENTS

C MF member Andrew Drain was a high-flying cardiothoracic surgeon working as a Fellow in a prestigious hospital in New York before becoming a consultant in the UK. In September 2007 he was diagnosed with the worst form of acute lymphoblastic leukaemia. Recovering with chemotherapy in New York, he returned to Ireland to have a bone marrow transplant.

Initially seeming to be cured, his final relapse began in June 2009. During remission he preached a series of sermons on the Bible's book of Job, his personal experiences illuminating his understanding of suffering.

Out of the blue the CMF Office received these sermons in written form in February 2010 and after discussion Andrew agreed to revise them by adding more details of his particular illness journey and by tentatively offering some advice to patients and to their carers.

He rapidly submitted another manuscript of almost equal length, and it has been my privilege to try to merge the two. The words that follow are almost entirely Andrew's. All responsibility for the editorial process is mine, although Andrew approved the final version weeks before he died peacefully at home on 3 July 2010.

Andrew Fergusson
Head of Communications
Christian Medical Fellowship

This is a book about pain, suffering and struggle; both Job's pain and the pain endured by Andy, Ruth and their family. Why would anyone want to read it? Or, come to that, why is the book of Job in the Bible in the first place?

One reason, I suppose, is our need to make sense of pain, both of our own and that of those around us. We want to be able to say something more profound than: 'life hurts, get used to it'. But we are also aware that some of the very noblest and richest lives turn out to be those lived in defiance of pain and suffering. There are men and women who, despite struggle, finally find a way to rise above their struggles.

This also fits with our suspicion that the significant turning points in our lives aren't found in the way we meet our pleasures, but in the way we face our pains. For the Christian, of course, all this is also reinforced by our understanding that *the* great achievement of Christ is to be found in the way he suffered.

Pleasure is a great gift, but it isn't a great teacher. Pain, meanwhile, while never welcome, often has the richest things to teach us. That's what this book is about. About the wisdom that comes from pain - Job's wisdom and the wisdom Andy gained during his illness. But this journey doesn't begin there. It starts with the perspective on suffering that Andy and Ruth had in place before trouble came.

In the twelve months before Andy and Ruth left Cambridge for New York, we had two sermon series on the subject of suffering. One was a topical series with the rather pompous title 'a theology of suffering'; the other was based on the life of Joseph described in the book of Genesis. Looking back it does seem extraordinarily bad planning to have scheduled two such similar series so close together. Yet less than a year later, Andy and Ruth described those talks as one of the many ways they felt God had prepared them for what was to come. God's planning, as usual, was rather better than ours.

The Bible's teaching about suffering is like prophylactic medicine – best administered in advance. In the midst of pain most of us would prefer an arm round the shoulder to a theological treatise. That is why we need the Bible's perspective on suffering in place *before* trouble strikes. What makes the book of Job so helpful is that it forces us to locate suffering on a much bigger canvas, on a canvas that has made room for God.

At least three things are distinctive about this book.

First, Andy knows his subject from the inside. A successful cardiac surgeon, with a thriving family he had, as they say, 'the world at his feet'. Chapter 3 describes the day Andy changed from surgeon to patient, from Thoracic Fellow to terminally ill. That he relates events that took place that day with a wry sense of humour tells you something of the journey he has subsequently travelled.

Secondly, he describes this experience as a doctor, and as a doctor married to a doctor! That doesn't just make his observations more perceptive, but gives them much added poignancy for those involved in 'the caring professions'. In the final chapter he gives a range of concluding 'reflections' about the way we talk to, and care for, those facing life-threatening illness. Knowing from his own experience how 'appropriate professional distance' can so easily drift into emotional indifference, his reflections will be of great help to those trying not to become hardened to the suffering of those they care for.

But the main reason his reflections are so helpful isn't to do with Andy at all. It has to do with the God who sustained him. It is the book of Job that Andy wants people to read; and the God of Job that Andy wants people to encounter. It took a little persuasion to get Andy to 'tell his story' in order that it could be woven into this account. He never wanted attention directed to him and his illness; he simply wanted to write about his God.

Early in his illness, knowing his chances of survival were slim, Andy began to plan his funeral. His first instruction was that the service must be 'less about me and more about God'. His ambition for this book is no different. At its heart are three sermons Andy wrote on the book of Job. He preached them in remission, wondering if perhaps he might be cured of his leukaemia; he edited them after a relapse, wondering how long he had to live. Of course that gives them extra poignancy. But in another sense everyone who reads (or preaches) the book of Job is *en route* to death. Death is always coming, however much we pretend otherwise. But what I have noticed is that Andy's willingness to confront the reality of his approaching death gave him a new freedom to live. And what these pages describe is the way his faith in Christ achieved that. Whether you read as sceptic or believer, this book offers a perspective on suffering that is life-changing. Not because Andy has arrived at astonishing new insights but because he shows us what is there in the Bible, and then shows us how he lived it out in his own life.

It has been a great privilege for me to stand with Andy and Ruth through the past few years. It has been a great joy to spend time with them and their children - though I never did win a single game of garden cricket. It may sound trite to say that during those visits they always gave me much more than I ever gave them, but it is true. Time spent with them has always left me spiritually stronger and more determined to live wholeheartedly for Christ. My prayer is that this will also be your experience as you read this account of God's dealings with Job and God's dealing with my friends.

Shortly before this book was finished Andy accepted an invitation to preach for us one more time at Christ Church. He spoke powerfully from James about being doers of the word and not hearers only (James 1:22). By God's grace Andy was a doer of the word and not a hearer only. By God's grace he received 'the implanted word, which is able to save your souls' (James 1:21). Andy hoped this book would direct others to the God of the Bible in order that they too would have confidence to say 'my Redeemer lives'.

Steve Midgley
worked in general practice and psychiatry before he was ordained. He is now Vicar of Christ Church, Cambridge

DEDICATION

This book is dedicated to Ruth, Josh, Conor and Olivia

n January 2009 I was asked to give a short series of sermons. I chose the book of Job, naively thinking that having battled leukaemia I was more qualified to speak on suffering than I really was. Despite my shortsightedness in attempting to preach one of the least understood books of the entire Bible, I was encouraged by others to put the sermons I had given into print.

When I gave my sermons on Job I didn't want them to be about me. I still don't. However, I have been encouraged and convinced that in order to draw the reader of this book more deeply into the story of Job (and ultimately thereby into the Lord Jesus of whom Job is in a sense a 'prototype') I should interweave the sermons with a 'brush-stroke' view of some of my own story. This should not only make the sermons more authentic, but might allow the reader to relate to the background from which I approach the book of Job, the Bible, and the whole issue of suffering.

In doing so, however, I want to make several things clear from the outset.

This is not a commentary on Job. This is not even an attempt to be scholarly or academic. Many excellent commentaries have been written, and will continue to be written, on Job. This is not an attempt to add to them. My recommendation for further reading is an excellent and highly readable commentary, *Out of the Storm*, by Christopher Ash. [1]

This is not an attempt to provide any intellectually or philosophically satisfying answers to human suffering. Whether or not such answers can even be derived from Job will continue to challenge all who look for them.

1.   Christopher Ash. *Out of the Storm. Questions and Consolations from the Book of Job*. IVP, 2004

I recognise that the spoken word is different from the written word. What follows in 'the Job sections' are sermons mainly as I preached them, and I would appreciate you making the appropriate allowances for this.

Above all, this is not the Bible. I hope it is biblical. I hope it is helpful. I trust that having all Bible references in full enables a clearer understanding of the sermons. However, nothing takes the place of reading the word of God, and I would encourage anyone to read the entire book of Job itself.

Soli Deo Gloria

INTRODUCTION

Life on earth is merely preparation for life in eternity. And while eternity excites me and scares me at the same time... we must remember that what Jesus offers is a new perspective in death not just in life

DAVID WATSON [2]

I was ten years old. It was a Sunday morning in February and we had just arrived home from church. I was still sliding on some ice on the front driveway when I saw dad at the front door. 'Kevin's dead', he said, tears streaming down his face. I was stunned. I had only met Kevin less than five times but he was one of my 'cool' older cousins. He was 17. He squeezed me onto the corkscrew rollercoaster at Alton Towers when I was too short to make the height requirement. He was a great footballer. He couldn't be dead, I thought. Kevin had gone to bed on the Saturday night and had never woken up. No cause was ever found.

I remember the day of the funeral as well. When the coffin came mum kept whispering to me: 'Kevin's not in there, he's in heaven'. It was comforting. The funeral was huge. I'd never been to one before. It was also very emotional. We sang 'Safe in the arms of Jesus' with no accompaniment. But it all seemed so surreal, particularly the coffin. All the crying, all the flowers, all the people. As a ten-year-old that strange couple of weeks did leave an impact on me. The fact I can remember so much of it 25 years later reinforces that. But essentially life very quickly returned to normal.

---

2. David Watson. BBC Radio. April 1983

Almost ten years later I saw my first dead body. I took a gap year before university with the mission then called Africa Evangelical Fellowship. I was seconded to a German mission in rural Tanzania, principally to teach music in a local school. As I was going to be returning to medical school, I was offered the opportunity to spend a couple of weeks in a mission hospital during some of my time off.

The baby was only a few months old but had acute cerebral malaria. I was given the task of holding the baby tightly flexed (curled round) to help the doctor carry out a lumbar puncture. Despite our efforts the child was dead within hours, and the public display of grief by the mother haunted me for weeks. As I looked at the lifeless form still held in the mother's arms I remembered what my mum had told me at Kevin's funeral: 'he's not in there, he's in heaven'. Despite this, it still all seemed surreal. There was crying, but this time there was no coffin, no other people, and no flowers.

As a cardiothoracic surgeon I dealt with death almost on a daily basis. I think I dealt with it candidly and objectively, regularly breaking the news of death to relatives, and rarely becoming emotionally involved. Yet when my three-year-old son had his tonsils out I worried intensely at what might happen under anaesthetic – that one-in-however-many-million risk that the tabloids remind us of every few years. I don't say this to defend my attitude at work, but to contrast it with my irrational fears when even the thought of death, however unlikely, was brought closer to home.

Death – my death – is one of the few certainties in life. Yet as a society we have never been less prepared to meet this appointed destiny. We live in a youth-orientated, health-worshipping, death-denying society. This means that death is 'all right' at arm's length. In fact we're fascinated by it when it's in a book, on a film, or in the news. But when it comes home to *our* family, to *our* place of work, to *our* neighbour, and to *us*, well that is an entirely different matter. We deny it, we turn away, we cross the road, we pass by on the other side.

But the fact that we shall all die should cause us to reflect on life, not just death. If we believe that life originated in a chance occurrence millions of years ago and is ultimately meaningless, then death is ultimately meaningless as well. Many Western writers and poets have stressed the futility of life without God, like Hemingway who comments that 'life is just a dirty trick, a short journey from nothingness to nothingness'. [3]

But when confronted by our death, our comfortable assumptions about our life are often found wanting. Is life really just 'an indefinite waiting for an explanation that never comes' (Samuel Beckett [4])? A naive belief that man is born with a guarantee of 'three score years and ten', that death is never today but always in the future, is seen to be without foundation.

As Christians we need to avoid a life perspective that is dependent on good physical health. But it is still natural to fear death and the manner of our dying. Canon David Watson, when he was ill with cancer, emphasised that the emotions take time to catch up with the intellect. He identified, from a Christian perspective, the radical change that is necessary, from (intellectually) willing to be in heaven but (emotionally) wanting to be on earth, to wanting to be in heaven but willing to stay on earth...until death comes.

Watson also distinguished between the fear of death and the fear of the process of dying. I can now really relate to that. When talking about death the 'theory' can seem so rehearsed. But when 'dying' we tread unfamiliar territory. We are uncertain and unsure. Facing up to the prospect of one's own death – not theoretically but in reality – is profoundly disturbing. That does not imply a lack of faith.

But as Christians we can be in no doubt as to our intended destiny. It is not some hazy afterlife but 'Real Life'. The teaching of the New Testament is unequivocal: this life is the shadow, the solid is to come. But while that hope fills us with a glorious peace about the future, the physical process of getting there can be frightening and painful.

Perhaps you're not a Christian. I remember giving a talk in Cambridge on 'Dignity in dying: will assisted suicide help?' I initially thought it would seem very contrived to squeeze the gospel into a talk which was essentially about euthanasia. But as I prepared the philosophical and ethical considerations surrounding euthanasia, I felt more and more compelled to convey the truth that *any* hope or peace in death will only come if we have a hope and vision of eternity; ie if we have a gospel-shaped view of life *and* death. The gospel of Jesus Christ transforms life, he transforms sickness, he transforms persistent ill health, he transforms old age, he transforms death, he transforms the process of dying. The

3. Quoted by Robert Twycross. *A Time to Die*. CMF, 1984
4. Samuel Beckett. *Waiting for Godot*. Faber and Faber, 2006

gospel must transform our attitude to, and perspective on, everything. God valued human life so much that he sent Jesus, who went through death on the worst possible level. As God and man he was stripped of all dignity; he was beaten, mocked and jeered, crucified naked, and left bleeding for all to see. But he died so we would have a hope and a certainty that death is not the end but the beginning.

The apostle Paul says that 'to live is Christ, and to die is gain' (Philippians 1:21). Why is this? Because for those who know Jesus, when we die we will be with him for ever. Does that mean we speed death's coming? That we precipitate it? No. But it does mean that our perspective must be one of wanting to be in heaven but willing to stay on earth, until his purposes for us have been fulfilled. Whatever our individual or collective suffering, the Christian gospel dictates that our hope extends not just to life, but to eternity, through the certain hope of resurrection and of restoration.

Death - my death - is one of the few certainties in life. But as I face 'the final enemy' I hold onto the words of the apostle Paul:

...the time of my departure has come. I have fought the good fight, I have finished the race, I have kept the faith. Henceforth there is laid up for me the crown of righteousness, which the Lord, the righteous judge, will award to me on that Day...

2 TIMOTHY 4:6-8

1

MY BACKGROUND

When you were born you cried and the world rejoiced.
Live your life in such a manner that when you die
the world cries and you rejoice

INDIAN PROVERB

GROWING UP

I was born into a Christian family on 9 June 1974; the same year as
the 'Rumble in the Jungle' when Muhammad Ali knocked out George
Foreman in eight rounds to regain the world heavyweight boxing title;
the same year Tim Henman, Robbie Williams, Victoria Beckham, and Ruth
Humphreys were born; the same year Duke Ellington, one of the greatest
jazz musicians ever, died. The year 1974 started on a Tuesday, I got
married on a Tuesday, and it was on Tuesday, 18 September 2007
that my life would change forever.

My parents are both strong Christians who brought up my two older
brothers and me under sound biblical principles, instruction and teaching.
Both sets of grandparents were Christians and both of my grandfathers
were full time Bible teachers. While I can't remember the exact date when
I became a Christian, I do not remember a time when I did not believe the
gospel as revealed in the Bible.

My childhood was very happy. I had very loving and supportive parents.
We lived in a nice house and I went to good schools. However, three things
of particular significance stand out from my school days, things I would
later reflect on during my treatment for leukaemia.

The first is that I genuinely loved my time at school – Sullivan Upper School, Holywood, in Northern Ireland. I was into everything and particularly loved sport (especially rugby), music and acting. Although I always wanted to do medicine I loved languages and history more than the sciences. I wasn't exceptional at anything but dabbled in almost everything the school had to offer. The enjoyment I got from it all gave me a quiet confidence that served me well for many years after leaving school.

Secondly, there were the friends I made at school, including many teachers who I still keep in touch with. Literally thousands of people from hundreds of churches have been praying for me and my family since I was diagnosed. The response was, and is, completely overwhelming and humbling, and Ruth and I are extremely appreciative of it. However, on hearing my diagnosis, one of my closest friends back in Northern Ireland started a weekly prayer meeting with ten other close friends. Despite university and 17 years of moving counties, countries, and continents, eight of the prayer group were friends I had made at Sullivan Upper School.

The third thing that stands out is the faithful, focused and inspiring leadership and prayer life of the Vice-Principal and head of the Scripture Union, Stanley Mills. His work within the SU was a life of sacrificial example that has influenced me hugely over the years. He prayed for 'revival' in Sullivan and one year (his *annus mirabilis*) some 100 pupils became Christians. I remember attending prayer meetings in his house 20 years ago where we prayed fervently for his 'dying' church where the congregation at times dwindled to single figures. I lost touch with those prayer meetings but he didn't. The same church now has a weekly attendance in the hundreds and is one of the fastest growing churches in Northern Ireland.

Why tell you all this? It is bad to dwell excessively on the past (or to plan excessively for the future) but I consider myself extremely privileged in the childhood and schooling I had. As I later would lie for days and weeks without the energy and concentration to read, talk or even watch TV, I found reminiscing about my school days enjoyable and uplifting, rather than introspective and depressing. I found knowing my best friends were still praying for me encouraging, and I knew Stanley Mills would be on his knees for me in prayer on a daily basis. But in my morphine-induced fog,

I was still able to appreciate just how privileged I had been in the school I had attended and the memories I still had from those days. I know that not everyone has equally good memories or experiences of school, and I mention these details to lay some context for my story rather than to assume my childhood as the norm.

UNIVERSITY

I had always intended to go away to university. However, ironically it was because I loved travelling that I didn't. Having taken a gap year in Tanzania and Mauritius, I thought staying in Belfast would give me more resources to travel in the long summer holidays. I spent one summer working with IFES (the International Fellowship of Evangelical Students) in Paris, another in the Middle East, and my medical student elective in South Africa and Zimbabwe. But like school there are several particular areas that stand out from my college days as being significant, both in terms of my personal development and my spiritual growth.

The first is that I met Ruth Olivia Humphreys. It was the first day of our first year. She was attractive, good fun, a Christian, and we became best friends from then on. I certainly didn't know on that particular day that in the course of time I would fall in love with her, ask her out (romantically – or as a complete 'saddo' – on Valentine's Day!), and ultimately marry her. As young undergraduates you believe you'll live for ever and life is just a seemingly endless sea of opportunity and possibilities. At that stage it is, and the optimistic enthusiasm and idealism of students I have always found refreshing whether in church, medicine or elsewhere.

The second is that I was Boarding Master in a large boarding school for three of my college years. The school was situated right in the middle of campus. I enjoyed the relationships you could develop with the boarders, particularly the large number from Malaysia who didn't go home at weekends. I enjoyed the team feeling among the Boarding Masters (15 in total) who all got on well and spent a lot of time together. I also enjoyed the free accommodation. But I look back on my time there, particularly in relation to the pupils, and feel some degree of shame. I was in a very influential position but was very ineffective in using the opportunity to share the gospel with both the boarders and staff. For sure they knew I was a Christian but to some extent it was a wonderful opportunity that I missed, or at least didn't fully maximise. I think in some ways because of that, and specifically because I reflected a lot on those years during my many inpatient sojourns, I now have more of a sense of urgency to reach people than I have ever had previously, and it's not purely because of my leukaemia.

Thirdly, Queen's University Belfast has a long tradition of a strong Christian Union. During my years at Queen's this was no different and the main meeting would have attracted several hundred undergrads each week. I was medical rep in my second year and also became involved with the music for the main campus meetings. In the middle of my second year the Executive invited me to be considered for President of the CU the following year. I deliberated for some time and eventually said no. I did have some ideas, and even a 'vision' as to which direction I felt the CU should be going. I would have liked to be President for many selfish reasons as well. But I had also been asked to consider taking charge of the music. I convinced myself that while there were several others who would make a great CU president (far better than me) I couldn't identify a suitable replacement to lead the praise and music. I accepted the role of music co-ordinator and initially felt justified in my decision. But I knew I had suppressed the main reason for my decision which had nothing to do with ministry or music…

I loved studying medicine. All of it intrigued and fascinated me. But as I got deeper into medical school I noticed the development (or unleashing!) of a driven, ambitious, competitive side of me that had been much quieter at school. I always liked to do well but at university it became so much more important to me. The truth about the CU presidency is that while I formulated well-sounding reasons for saying no, and even believed them, deeper down I knew how much work would be involved and was concerned how it might affect my studies. Essentially, I got my priorities wrong. It was a decision I should have made differently in hindsight, but it was also a decision that started a trend of getting my priorities wrong that I would struggle with for years.

CAMBRIDGE

After university I still had the travel bug. For those who enjoy travel I don't think it ever fully leaves, it just changes form. So towards the end of my house officer year I applied for surgical training in Cambridge. I knew Cambridge. I knew it was a beautiful city and at that stage academia also interested me, or at least the thought of it did. I knew Grantchester, an idyllic village within puntable distance of Cambridge. Although I don't share his views it was in Grantchester that Rupert Brooke wrote much of his poetry, including 'for Cambridge people rarely smile, being urban, squat, and packed with guile'!

I initially planned to go for two years but after SHO jobs I arranged to stay on to do a PhD. Prior to starting the research a specialist registrar (SpR) training post came up in cardiothoracic surgery and the pull to my first love of operating quickly overcame any aspirations of academic prowess. Two years in Cambridge turned into eight. I loved cardiac surgery. I loved Papworth and I was very happy. However, during those eight years, three things and six people became a part of my life that would change it in a positive way forever, and for which I have been even more grateful since being diagnosed with leukaemia.

The first is that I got married. Ruth joined me the summer after I went to Cambridge and we were married on 29 August 2000, the year of the Millennium. I carried her over the threshold of a one-bedroom hospital flat which would be ours for the next 15 months. It was small and cramped. It was noisy and *everything* from the surrounding flats could be heard without effort. It had a hospital accommodation 'grime' that never quite went away. The bed was broken, sloped in the middle like a 'V' and despite being newly weds this was not a good shape! But we loved our first digs, and the living room floor saw more friends and visitors than I can begin to remember. Ruth is amazing; most importantly a woman of faith, but also with pragmatism, strength, and a great sense of humour. We didn't however realise just how much we would come to rely on those particular attributes further down the line.

The second is that all our children were born in Cambridge. Josh, Conor and Olivia spent their first few years sitting on the back of our bikes, chasing the cows in Midsummer Common, running through the leaves in Jesus Green, or being punted on the Cam. They were, and are, an amazing source of love, joy and potential! We consider ourselves immensely blessed and rejoice in these three precious gifts. But as I will discuss later, while they are one of the greatest sources of our happiness, leaving them for weeks on end for various treatments, and as I currently have to reconcile leaving them again when I am finally called home, is without doubt one of the most difficult challenges of the whole sickness. I love them so much.

The third is my personal spiritual growth. In 2001 I took time out of medicine to spend two months working at St Andrew the Great (StAG), the largest student-orientated church in Cambridge. But before sounding too virtuous, Ruth and I had just spent the previous two months touring Hong Kong and the Antipodes. My specialist training in Papworth had already been secured, including permission for a short sabbatical before starting. So I wasn't doing it with any great leap of faith – I knew my training pathway was not affected. Having been a very active Christian at school and university, like many junior doctors I had spent the next few years just about breaking even on spiritual terms and certainly not offering much in terms of service. Mainly under the influence and mentorship of Mark Ashton and Simon Scott, my time at StAG turned out to be one of the best and most concentrated times of spiritual growth that I had ever had and set me on a course from which I have never really looked back. I continued at StAG on the student and music team, and with Ruth on the marriage team for a further 18 months. My time there re-taught me many things: the absolute importance of biblical authority, the centrality of the Word in all that we do, the significance of personal contact, and that a great vicar can still laugh when the main stained glass window at the front of the church gets smashed by a stray football!

It was also at StAG that we first came across Steve and Beth Midgley. They headed the marriage team and were a couple who would become a much bigger part of our lives over the next few years, and even more so in the years after we left Cambridge. Steve had been a doctor before going into ordained ministry – something I had been thinking about for a (very!) long time. In 2003 Steve and Beth led a church plant from StAG to Christ Church Cambridge. We signed up and Ruth and I became heavily involved. We still have many close friends from there and almost three years after having left we still consider Christ Church in many ways as 'home'. It is certainly the place where our marriage and our children enjoyed their formative years and it is with immense gratitude and honour that I remember our time there.

The Lord gave, and the Lord has taken away;
blessed be the name of the Lord.

JOB 1:21

I once saw a drama on BBC1 about a Northern Ireland ex-paramilitary who was involved in a reconciliation process. In the opening scene he began by saying, 'I'm going to tell you about the man I have become, but first I must tell you about the man I was'. The writer of Job could very easily have started his book the same way. Like the ex-paramilitary, to understand Job fully at the end of the book, and who he became in his suffering, the book opens by telling us who he was.

PROLOGUE:
THE SERVANT, THE SETTING AND THE GLIMPSE INTO HEAVEN

Have you considered my servant Job?

JOB 1:8

The book of Job is set out as a poem or story with three dialogues. The first is between God and Satan in chapters 1-2, the second between Job and his 'friends' in chapters 3-37, and the third between Job and his God in chapters 38-42. In chapter 1, before the dialogue between God and Satan, we are introduced to Job and his character.

Job was 'blameless [not claiming to be sinless, but a genuine believer who continues to walk with God with no unrepented sin - Christopher Ash [5]] and upright, one who feared God and turned away from evil' (v1). If suffering is intended as a punishment for evil, as Job's friends claim in the following chapters, then Job is not a very likely candidate. His 'righteousness' was legendary (see Ezekiel 14:14). 'Have you considered my servant Job?' can actually be seen as a great compliment.

Secondly, Job was very, very rich. 'He possessed 7,000 sheep, 3,000 camels, 500 yoke of oxen, and 500 female donkeys, and very many servants, so that this man was the greatest of all the people of the east' (v3). Job was the Bill Gates of the East. If money could somehow insure you against suffering, Job could have paid the highest premium and still had some left over to buy his wife a convertible! Earthly wealth is of no value when we are considering things of heavenly importance.

Thirdly, Job was a devout family man:

His sons used to go and hold a feast in the house of each one on his day, and they would send and invite their three sisters to eat and drink with them. And when the days of the feast had run their course, Job would send and consecrate them, and he would rise early in the morning and offer burnt offerings according to the number of them all. For Job said, 'It may be that my children have sinned, and cursed God in their hearts.' (1:4-5)

These verses allow us to look at his life to see his reverence for God and his love for his family. Job cared for his family and he cared about their relationship with God. Then, seemingly out of nowhere, disaster came:

Now there was a day when his sons and daughters were eating and drinking wine in their oldest brother's house, and there came a messenger to Job and said, 'The oxen were ploughing and the donkeys feeding beside them, and the Sabeans fell upon them and took them and struck down the servants with the edge of the sword, and I alone have escaped to tell you.' While he was yet speaking, there came another and said, 'The fire of God fell from heaven and burned up the sheep and the servants and consumed them, and I alone have escaped to tell you.' While he was yet speaking, there came another and said, 'The Chaldeans formed three groups and made a raid on the camels and took them and struck down the

---

5. Christopher Ash. *Out of the Storm. Questions and Consolations from the Book of Job*. IVP, 2004. p17

servants with the edge of the sword, and I alone have escaped to tell you.'
While he was yet speaking, there came another and said, 'Your sons and
daughters were eating and drinking wine in their oldest brother's house,
and behold, a great wind came across the wilderness and struck the four
corners of the house, and it fell upon the young people, and they are
dead, and I alone have escaped to tell you.' (1:13-19)

All his prosperity, his livestock and servants are stolen or killed and all ten
of Job's children are crushed to death in one afternoon. Can most of us
even begin to imagine the pain and loss Job experienced in that one
afternoon? What in the world is going on? But to see what's going on we
can't look in the world. We will never get an answer in the world. But the
writer of Job, inspired by God, gives us a snapshot, a glimpse into heaven
so that we can see what is going on:

Now there was a day when the sons of God came to present themselves
before the Lord, and Satan also came among them. The Lord said to
Satan, 'From where have you come?' Satan answered the Lord and said,
'From going to and fro on the earth, and from walking up and down on it.'
And the Lord said to Satan, 'Have you considered my servant Job, that
there is none like him on the earth, a blameless and upright man, who
fears God and turns away from evil?' Then Satan answered the Lord and
said, 'Does Job fear God for no reason? Have you not put a hedge around
him and his house and all that he has, on every side? You have blessed
the work of his hands, and his possessions have increased in the land. But
stretch out your hand and touch all that he has, and he will curse you to
your face.' And the Lord said to Satan, 'Behold, all that he has is in your
hand. Only against him do not stretch out your hand.' So Satan went out
from the presence of the Lord. (1:6-12)

Now I will admit that I don't completely understand this meeting. Why is
it allowed? Was it after Satan had been thrown out of heaven? But then
how did he get access to heaven? How is he permitted such an audience
with the Almighty? I don't know. But like much of Job, we are asked to
deal with and apply what we do know, rather than worry about what
we aren't told or don't know or don't understand.

In v9 Satan suggests that Job is perhaps not as good as God thinks:
'Does Job fear God for no reason?' Who wouldn't like God if he gets lots
of blessings in return? Satan claims Job is in it purely and selfishly for

what he gets out of it. Take away what you have given him, his wealth and his family and he will curse you (v11). Satan is not just concerned with Job, but he is also challenging God's assessment of Job.

God didn't need to prove anything to Satan. Just as when Jesus was tempted in the wilderness he dismissed Satan with his knowledge of scripture, so God could easily have dismissed Satan. But for whatever reason, this time he chose not to. Instead, God allows Satan's claim to stand, at least temporarily, in order to display that in the heart of Job, God's chosen servant, God himself is of paramount value, not the blessings he has received from God.

Then unprovoked, unmerited (at least to those on earth), and with no warning, major disaster strikes as has been permitted by God, not Satan. But despite the enormity of the scale of Job's suffering he does not deny his God. Satan fails and a great heavenly victory is recorded:

Then Job arose and tore his robe and shaved his head and fell on the ground and worshipped. And he said, 'Naked I came from my mother's womb, and naked shall I return. The Lord gave, and the Lord has taken away; blessed be the name of the Lord.' In all this Job did not sin or charge God with wrong. (1:20-21)

Satan's power is exposed as being very limited. Satan was wrong. Job did not curse God when he lost his wealth, his possessions and his children. Job had stood firm. He had held onto his faith and worshipped God. But just as he was recovering from the shock of losing it all he looks down at his hands and notices something new:

So Satan went out from the presence of the Lord and struck Job with loathsome sores from the sole of his foot to the crown of his head. And he took a piece of broken pottery with which to scrape himself while he sat in the ashes. (2:7-8)

This isn't a mild skin disease or a bad case of acne. This is a gross, body-covering, chronic, disgusting skin problem. I'm not sensationalising it:

...so I am allotted months of emptiness, and nights of misery are apportioned to me. When I lie down I say, 'When shall I arise?' But the night is long, and I am full of tossing till the dawn. My flesh is clothed

with worms and dirt; my skin hardens, then breaks out afresh. (7:3-5)

This was a chronic skin disease allowing Job no peace, no sleep, no healing; and he hated it:

My breath is strange to my wife, and I am a stench to the children of my own mother. Even young children despise me; when I rise they talk against me. All my intimate friends abhor me, and those whom I loved have turned against me. My bones stick to my skin and to my flesh, and I have escaped by the skin of my teeth. (19:17-20)

What in the world is going on? Surely Job had done so well? Once more, I don't fully understand it but the writer again shows us we'll never find out what's happening if we look in the world, and so he gives us another glimpse into heaven:

Again there was a day when the sons of God came to present themselves before the Lord, and Satan also came among them to present himself before the Lord. And the Lord said to Satan, 'From where have you come?' Satan answered the Lord and said, 'From going to and fro on the earth, and from walking up and down on it.' And the Lord said to Satan, 'Have you considered my servant Job, that there is none like him on the earth, a blameless and upright man, who fears God and turns away from evil? He still holds fast his integrity, although you incited me against him to destroy him without reason.' Then Satan answered the Lord and said, 'Skin for skin! All that a man has he will give for his life. But stretch out your hand and touch his bone and his flesh, and he will curse you to your face.' And the Lord said to Satan, 'Behold, he is in your hand; only spare his life.' (2:1-6)

Again God allows Job to be attacked by Satan. However difficult it is, the Bible gives us no assurance that current suffering will protect us from future suffering. The opening chapters of Job force us to distinguish the difference between the 'now' and the 'not yet'. For some this world will be full of suffering after suffering, and often there will be no obvious reason why. Some will die young. Others will be born into poverty or disability or disease. But as we work through Job we will experience the difference between what may happen to us 'now' and what is promised will be ours in the 'not yet'.

Again Satan has challenged the authenticity of Job's worship. Again the worth of God is challenged. Is God in himself what Job values? Or is it the health that God gives? Does Job love God or his gifts? Verse 6 shows us that behind these apparently absurd, undeserved, unmerited experiences of suffering, something is going on in heaven of universal significance. When God confers with or allows Satan to challenge his servants something huge must be at stake! The very honour and glory of the Almighty is being challenged by Satan through his accusations of Job.

I wonder: do you believe that how you respond to God in your problems, in your suffering, is of huge significance and importance to God? For God what is important is whether his children reverence him, and hold on to their faith *in* their time of suffering. When God chooses to allow his arch enemy into the halls of heaven, and then gives him permission to attack, however difficult we find that to understand, then something of heavenly, universal significance is taking place.

Then his [Job's] wife said to him, 'Do you still hold fast your integrity? Curse God and die.' But he said to her, 'You speak as one of the foolish women would speak. Shall we receive good from God, and shall we not receive evil?' In all this Job did not sin with his lips. (2:9-10)

Imagine Satan awaiting Job's next action: 'Fair enough, Job gave a pretty good response to losing his wealth and children with this "the Lord gives and the Lord takes away thing, blessed be the name of the Lord"...but now I've got the children, the wealth, the health and now probably the wife too (v9-10), there's no way he won't curse God this time'. But Job stays faithful 'and in all this Job did not sin with his lips' (v10). God had won again!

So we have set the scene for the rest of the book of Job. Chapters 1 and 2 allow us a vantage point Job never received. But I believe our opening scenes also highlight and reaffirm three things about suffering that must guide all our other thoughts. These are God's permission, God's protection, and God's perspective.

The book of Job deals with suffering, but perhaps never fully answers the questions we might ask. At least if it does, the answers are complex and multifaceted. There are no nice, neatly packaged, boxed up answers. No nutshell message of the book of Job. And so my prayer is that our understanding of suffering will evolve and expand and be experienced, rather than be dictated and prescribed as we go through Job.

To try and turn Job into a set of principles would violate what the book teaches about the mysteries of God's working in the lives of his people. With that in mind, let's see if we can apply Job generally.

GOD'S PERMISSION

'God does grant to Satan limited power but limited only to accomplish the opposite of what Satan intended' (John Piper).[6] God grants to Satan limited power to cause pain: '...all that he has is in your hand. Only against him do not stretch out your hand' (1:12); '...he is in your hand; only spare his life' (2:6). God's condition in allowing Satan to inflict Job is that he spares his life. It is a condition Job and others after him may have wished God had not imposed. But we should note that Satan can do nothing except with God's permission. It is a twist and biblical distortion to give Satan more power than he has.

One commentator writes: 'Satan may be a lion, prowling around seeking who he may devour, but he is on a leash and God can rein him in or give him slack according to his own sovereign purposes'.[7]

We must reaffirm that God is totally sovereign. Satan's plan is ultimately reversed into God's work and God's plan. Notice in the two heavenly scenes it is God who first hands over Job to Satan. Satan grabs that power, thinking he has the edge. He takes Job's wealth, his possessions, and his family. But in 1:21, Job doesn't say *Satan* has taken away my sheep and my children, he says *the Lord* has 'taken away'. Job is not pious. He's not trying to super-spiritualise everything. Yet the hands that took Job's possessions and family *were* the hands of Satan. But what Job is saying is that the Lord's permission was in everything that happened. Despite this, despite believing God was actually in control of his suffering, still he says blessed, blessed, blessed be the name of the Lord, my sovereign king.

Similarly and even more pointedly in 2:7 Satan went forth from the presence of the Lord and afflicted Job (it was definitely Satan) yet in v10 Job appeals to his now doubting wife, 'shall we receive good from God and...not evil?' The root of Job's strength and faith is that he reaches

----

6. www.desiringgod.org/ResourceLibrary/Sermons/ByScripture/18/497_Job_Reverent_in_Suffering
7. Ibid.

behind Satan and reaches all the way up to the sovereignty of God, and can still see that in all things God reigns. Satan may have been the instrument through which calamity came to Job, but ultimately Job knows it was permitted by God.

Now I realise we may find this difficult, even surprising, that God is completely in control of our suffering. But I say it first because I believe the Bible teaches it, and also because I find it hugely comforting, not concerning or alarming. I find it encouraging that the Lord may not have planned my suffering, but by the time it reaches me it has completely got the Lord's permission.

Derek Bingham, a well known local Bible teacher and author, was diagnosed with leukaemia. When initially he recovered from the ill effects of treatment he said to me 'the doctors call it remission, but I say it is the Lord's permission!' And that is exactly the story of God's sovereignty in the book of Job.

GOD'S PROTECTION

God seeks followers who cling to him more than anything else. If our faith is indestructible in tribulation, if it holds firm in suffering, then his glory will shine to the rest of the world. Who wouldn't want a faith that is powerful enough to glow even more brightly through our suffering, not just shine when things are going well? The irony of chapters 1 and 2 is that ultimately God only allows Satan to accomplish the opposite of what Satan had intended. Satan intended God to be cursed by Job, to be shown up by his 'blameless' servant who Satan thought had made the good things 'God' things and only loved God because of what he received in return. But what Satan attempted, what God permitted, and how Job responded, actually resulted in God being worshipped.

Paul reminds the Corinthian church that God will not let us be tested beyond what we can bear (1 Corinthians 10:13). It's not a fight between God and Satan. God limits what Satan can do. Satan is on that leash. Of course as far as we know, Job knew none of this – and therefore his reaction is all the more mind-blowing. We will come back to the protection of God, but let us join Job in reaffirming God's sovereignty. Let's make God's sovereignty the rock on which we stand in the midst of our troubles. Let's take encouragement and hope, knowing that the Lord may not have planned our suffering but that by the time it reaches us it has completely got the Lord's permission and we have completely got the Lord's protection.

GOD'S PERSPECTIVE
Human nature dictates that we usually think we know what is best for us. We must review our mistaken perception of what God really wants for us. Just because we can't see or imagine a good reason why God might allow something to happen, it doesn't mean there can't be one. Remember God is God. His ways are not our ways and his thoughts are not our thoughts (Isaiah 55:8). We'll see this more when we look at Job chapter 28.

This is not intended to be a philosophical discussion of why God can be good and allow suffering, but seen through a mistaken concept of divine goodness and human happiness, many would see undeserved suffering as overwhelming evidence against the existence of any good or loving God. But for someone with a correct understanding of God's love, we can see that it is precisely because God loves us that he permits us to suffer.

For many, what makes human suffering so puzzling is that God is supposed to love us. But to explain God's love for humanity, CS Lewis draws a distinction between genuine love and mere kindness. The primary goal of kindness is a pleasant existence. A false conception of divine goodness is that it amounts to nothing more than God wanting us to live comfortable, pleasant, materially rewarding earthly lives.

But genuine divine goodness involves love rather than kindness, and while God's love clearly and biblically precedes our perfection (while we were still sinners Christ died for us - Romans 5:8), his love also desires that one day we would be perfect. God knows our human happiness can only truly be found in our becoming more Christ-like. If instead, however, we hold to our 'things' (our family, money, job, status and our desire to love them) more than to God, then the good things God has given us become ultimate things, and our suffering will separate us from these things, pulling us further away from them and making us sadder and madder and more bitter.

God gives us many good things that we are fully allowed to enjoy, but we must not depend on them. If however, our life is built on God - his ultimate love, his ultimate wealth - then suffering will actually drive us deeper into the very source of our joy, Jesus Christ our Lord.

CS Lewis (*The Problem of Pain*): 'Once we properly understand God's omnipotence and goodness, and the real nature of human happiness, we will see that it is not at all surprising or improbable that God would permit human suffering.'[8] Suffering is one of the tools God uses to transform us, to nudge us toward genuine happiness.

When we mistake the point of the world, and see it as only to produce pleasant, pleasure-filled lives, then we will stumble when good people suffer, and we will ask: what in the world is going on? But the book of Job and many other parts of the Bible clearly teach that God works in and through our suffering. He may not enjoy it. We certainly hate it. But when we understand God's true purpose for each one of us, then we can take confidence in our suffering knowing that *through* our suffering we are being moulded to be more like Christ. While there is no guarantee, occasionally, as we will see with Job, we may even be able to look back and see for ourselves that what has happened has happened for a very specific reason or purpose.

This, however, does not in any way mean that we have to smile when suffering comes (1:20). When we suffer we very rarely get the 'God's eye view' or are privy to why it's happening. Jesus' disciples didn't always get it. Moses didn't always understand. Jacob certainly struggled with God's perspective and while Joseph couldn't initially see it either, he came to realise that what was meant for his harm by some, God all along meant for his good (Genesis 50:20). But not being allowed God's view of what's happening is the only way we really learn to love God for who he is, and to trust him despite, not because. It is when we cling on through blood, sweat, toil and tears to the God who loves us through and in our suffering that we learn to love him for who he is.

Crying, being upset, being cross, and mourning are not signs of unbelief. That's okay. Job knows nothing of a flippant, insensitive, praise-God-anyhow response to suffering. The magnificence of Job's worship is that it was offered during his grief and not instead of grief. When your suffering comes, and it will come, don't be afraid not to smile! Don't be afraid to let the tears run down your cheeks until there are no more. And if you're the church elder, the spouse or the partner, or the friend or the pastor who is called to the bedside or the house or the living room of

8. CS Lewis. *The Problem of Pain*. (First published 1940.) London: Fount, 1998. Ch. 3 'Divine Goodness'

someone who is suffering, when it happens, please be slow to preach to them in their hour of need. When that moment comes, hold them if needed, cry with them if needed, but be very careful before you open your mouth with platitudes and well-known Bible verses. Although perhaps for the wrong reasons, Job's friends initially got it right (we'll see this later) when they just came and sat and wept and said nothing. There is a time to speak and we will look at that too, but initially we must just be there. When suffering comes, and it will seem meaningless, don't be afraid not to smile.

CONCLUSION

We usually go to the cross to talk about grace, and that is true, but grace is here right at the start of Job. If we go back to 1:20 we see it's not about stoicism, about gritting our teeth and a stiff upper lip. It's not about just keeping on going, but it's all about grace. We are naked and helpless and everything we have is from God.

So where do we go from here? Joe Bayly, in his ominously titled book *The view from a hearse* comments 'when you're not suffering then it is only intellectual. If you are suffering it becomes a journey.'[9] I don't know whether this is purely intellectual for you, or you're in a living hell and you wish I would just shut up and take my theology away from the real world of broken lives. But I hope you have seen through these opening chapters that God does grant to Satan only limited power. We must be confident and encouraged that God is totally sovereign. In addition we can also be sure of his total protection. Finally we must review our perception of what God really wants for us as we attempt to adopt and apply *his* perspective.

But Job also forces us to look ahead to him who underwent the ultimate unjust suffering. As if he needed it, Satan tried to give God proof that Job was only in it for what he got out of it. Satan was wrong. In our suffering we often cry out for proof that God really loves us. And yet do we really need any more proof that God loves us than what he has already given us? We have complete proof – in the Lord Jesus Christ. When Jesus Christ, the son of God, was crucified by a band of Roman soldiers, the ultimate undeserved, unmerited, and seemingly meaningless suffering took place.

---

9. Joseph Bayly. *The view from a hearse. A Christian view of death*. DC Cook Publishing company, 1973

Philosopher Peter Kreeft says the Christian God came to earth deliberately to 'put himself on the hook of human suffering'. Isaiah 53:10 tells us it was 'the will of the Lord to crush him' and to cause him to suffer. Yes, God permitted his son to undergo suffering on our behalf. In Jesus Christ, God himself experienced the greatest depths of pain. We don't always get a reason 'why' to explain each of our experiences of pain, but we are provided with a 'who' to help us face our suffering with hope rather than bitterness, courage rather than despair. On the cross Jesus went beyond even the worst human suffering, and experienced cosmic rejection and pain that exceeds ours as infinitely as his knowledge, love and power exceed ours.

And yet it was God allowing Satan just enough slack on his leash that demonstrated to us just how much God loves us and to Satan exactly who is in control. On the cross Jesus completed the ultimate defeat of evil and suffering so that we can never walk in darkness again. When Jesus rose from the dead he didn't 'depart naked', he rose triumphant, to be exalted at the right hand of God, to remind us that one day all suffering will cease for those who believe in him, all tears will be wiped away for those who make him their Lord, and all death has been conquered for those who submit their lives to him. In Job we begin to see Jesus, and must therefore fall on our knees in grateful thanks for the one who underwent the ultimate, undeserved suffering.

NEW YORK, AND BECOMING A LEUKAEMIA PATIENT

*It's ridiculous to set a detective story in New York City.
New York City is a detective story*

AGATHA CHRISTIE

I t had taken two and a half years of organising, nearly £3,000 of
United States Licensing Medical Exam (USLME) fees not to mention
the time involved studying for the exams, a trip to Chicago, a 5-day
interview process in New York, three months of almost nightly form-filling
to ensure medical licences arrived on time, and a very long day queuing
at the American Embassy in London. But now I was there!

Memorial Sloan-Kettering Cancer Center ('MSK') is situated in an
attractive residential area in the Upper East Side of Manhattan. Affiliated
with Cornell Medical School it is a dedicated cancer centre, one of the
biggest units in the USA and arguably the world. For thoracic surgery
it is particularly renowned and it was for that reason that I was there.

It was the end of June 2007 and I had come to New York alone, deciding
to leave my wife, Ruth, and the three children (Josh, Conor and Olivia) to
come later once I got established. The temperature was over 90 degrees
and the humidity higher, but as I walked into the hospital apartment, '13R,
63rd and York', I was blown away by the amazing panoramic view of the
East River. Not only the river but the Queensboro Bridge (which we
affectionately came to call the 'Spider-Man bridge' following its starring
role in the film), and the Franklin D Roosevelt Drive all seemed within
touching distance of our 13th floor apartment window. Months later Paula
Radcliffe would jog across the bridge on her way to winning the 2007
New York Marathon. I felt a sigh of relief. I had landed on my feet. Ruth

would be happy – the prospect of moving with three children to the heart of Manhattan was understandably daunting. But this was an incredible apartment, bigger than I expected, with excellent children's play areas, and with a view that I still consider one of the most memorable in my life.

The first month went really well. I loved the surgery. I loved the freedom I was being given to operate and the many friends, colleagues and patients I met made the time fly. There was a gym on the 38th floor of the apartment block with an unrivalled view out over the Manhattan skyline. Rather than just talk about it, and with no family out yet, for the month of July I actually used the gym and had never felt fitter. On the same floor there was also a large function room where I watched the 4th of July Independence Day fireworks and could easily see the huge laser beams that were projected into the sky from 'Ground Zero' on 11 September.

But I missed Ruth and the children. We phoned, texted and Skyped and eventually (or providentially!) agreed they should all come out earlier than planned. I squeezed in a few jazz concerts, a blue-grass banjo performance in Carnegie Hall (which I had mistakenly booked thinking it was jazz!), and spent the rest of the time trying to make the apartment perfect for their arrival.

Ruth, to the incredulity of just about everyone I spoke to, brought all three children (then four years, two years and four months) on the flight from Dublin to New York by herself! For seven weeks after they arrived we had some of the most fun family time we have ever had and despite now looking back with tinted spectacles, we still regard those weeks as among the most precious our family has spent together. Ruth had spent much of July going through travel books of New York with the boys, and so despite their age when they arrived they knew more about the tourist attractions than I did!

Every day Ruth would do something different with the children; Central Park (within which are 21 different children's play areas), the Natural History Museum, the Bronx Zoo, and even some of New York's most famous art galleries! The boys learned to hail the ubiquitous yellow taxis with ease while Ruth became an expert in managing three young children on the 'sidewalk'. Mid-week I worked long hours and was on call every night but at weekends, even on-call I could still go to most places in the Upper East Side, including Central Park. We ran through the sprinklers, had picnics on the Great Lawn, and did a lot of people watching. On Sundays we attended Redeemer church (a large church committed to church-planting and gospel renewal in New York City) then usually grabbed a Subway sandwich *en route* to Central Park. We made great friends and very quickly became settled in our Manhattan life. It was a children's dream. It was a parent's dream. Far from being a nightmare for children we found Manhattan, or more specifically the Upper East Side, to be one of the most child-friendly places we had ever been.

The summer had been brilliant; the 'Fall' would be equally brilliant. We had planned trips to Boston and New Hampshire and then there would be Christmas in New York – ice skating in Central Park and the famous Christmas tree at the Rockefeller Center. We would return to Cambridge having had a great time in New York, my CV would be enhanced, and it would just be a matter of time before the right consultant job would be placed on my lap. The next twelve months were pretty well sorted...'DV' of course!

'NOT QUITE SO FAST...'

I was becoming progressively more tired. By the beginning of September I would arrive home most nights somewhere between 7-9pm and fall asleep putting the children to bed or in front of the TV. Despite the satellite providing us with over 1,000 different channels and every sport conceivable (except the 2007 Rugby World Cup where Ireland had been predicted to do quite well!) it failed to keep me awake. Manhattan was still very hot and humid. I was working hard and in any spare time I always wanted to do 'family stuff'. So the tiredness was fully understandable.

I then began to develop a strange chest pain. It wasn't too annoying and was easily relieved by simple painkillers. Transferring patients in the Operating Room ('OR') was co-ordinated by the surgeon and so I had done a lot of heavy lifting. I had probably just developed a bit of muscle pain. I also woke up several nights in early September drenched in sweat but as we always left the air-conditioning off overnight, again it was fully explainable.

On Monday 3 September we returned to New York by train from a great weekend break in Washington. A week later, on Monday 10 September (Labor Day and a national holiday) one of my colleagues offered to cover my patients allowing me to take the family on an exciting adventure to Coney Island – the 'Blackpool' of New York. On Monday 17 September

I performed three lobectomies (for the removal of lung cancer) and was home by 7pm. But as the evening wore on my chest pain worsened. Was it actually chest or upper abdominal? Had I been taking too much ibuprofen and now developed a peptic ulcer? By 10pm I couldn't bear the pain and selfishly asked Ruth to head out into the Upper East Side night to find a pharmacy that was open. I needed something for the pain and something for what I thought was a probable ulcer. With a combination of painkillers and antacids I eventually drifted off to sleep...

I woke at 5am in complete agony. I could barely catch my breath or even walk due to a combination of chest and abdominal pain. Ruth was fast asleep as I had slept on the sofa in case I was called by work about a patient. She was very used to me leaving in the middle of the night but I woke her up to tell her I had to go to the 'ER' as I was in so much pain. I said it would be fine and I'd let her know how I got on once I was back in work.

MSK didn't have an Emergency facility for non-cancer patients who weren't already under their care. The hospital across the road, New York Presbyterian (NYP), did. I phoned Netu, one of my colleagues and the Chief Resident, to let him know I would be late for work and to ask if he would mind 'rounding' on my patients. Having previously worked in NYP during his training, Netu phoned the ER to tell them I was coming. By the time I had completed the ten minute walk from our apartment to the NYP-ER I was pale and sweaty and given I was complaining of chest pain I was fast tracked through the department at high speed. Within an hour my pain had been relieved (with 40 mg morphine!), I'd had a transthoracic echo (scan of the heart), ECG monitoring, a CT scan and more medical staff looking after me than a 'crash' scene from the TV series *ER*. Needless to say, Ruth was slightly surprised when the 'Attending' (consultant) from NYP phoned her at about 7am. 'Your husband is okay. We've ruled out a heart attack, an aortic dissection and a pulmonary embolism. We're just waiting on some blood tests to come back.'

Our experience of American kindness, selflessness and generosity has been amazing. It started the morning of my admission. Ruth emailed the other Fellows' wives in the apartment block at 7am to ask if anyone would mind looking after the children to allow her to call up to the ER. At 30 weeks pregnant and already with one child of her own, Kerri had been online and was at the door of 13R within minutes, still dressed in her PJs. 'Just go', she told Ruth.

Back in the ER most major things seemed to have been ruled out and my pain was much better, although still requiring intermittent morphine. But there was an uneasy quiet among the staff in my bay. They wanted more blood but strangely didn't tell me why. When I was left alone with one of the nurses I vividly remember asking her what the problem was. 'One of your blood tests is a bit abnormal', she said. 'They just want to recheck it.'

I've never liked vague answers, but particularly so in medicine. I pressed her and learned that the white cell count (the cells that fight infection, 'WCC') was 90. It should have been less than 10. I had seen several 'lab-errors' over the years but knew this was very unlikely to be one. Laboratories don't make those sorts of mistakes with white cell counts. The repeat blood test came back with a WCC of 74 and other results showing a serious failure of normal bone marrow function.

While the repeat blood tests were being processed Ruth had nipped back to check the children were okay. Somehow oblivious to what was actually happening, and not fully aware of the significance of the repeat tests, I texted Ruth the results. Ruth is a paediatrician. She had done paediatric oncology and haematology for over a year and knew exactly what the results meant. Looking back I still can't believe I told her by text message, but it seemed so appropriate at the time, 'just to let her know'.

Things then took on a rather unusual twist. Even before Ruth had managed to make it back to the ER, Netu arrived over from MSK, knew exactly what was happening and was adamant that my boss from MSK wanted me to be treated 'back across the road'. I didn't even know what was happening yet! Within minutes of Netu arriving the Grand Round of haematologists from NYP also descended into my emergency bay in the ER. The Attending was extremely warm but pulled no punches, something I have generally liked. 'You have acute leukaemia' he said, 'and will need emergency treatment'. I still remember my first question: 'Can I go back to the UK for it?' But the answer was no, I was too unwell.

I decided to receive my treatment in MSK not NYP. But a hospital transfer, even though it was literally across the road, would require a lot of paper work, an ambulance trip and a formal handover. I would remain in NYP most of the day as I was at this stage very unwell. But Netu, my 'hostage negotiator', had been given strict instructions by the bosses in MSK. It was a 'code red' for the Thoracic Fellow. His mission was to escort me back to MSK there and then, with as little collateral damage as possible, but as much as necessary for the mission to succeed. While the rounding haematology team of NYP went for their morning coffee, Netu acquired a wheelchair from the ER, put me in it, and wheeled me straight out of the emergency department of NYP. He wheeled me straight past the medical staff, the nursing staff, the reception staff and ultimately the security staff, with no paper work, no questions, and no looking back.

Ironically, the view from the room I would occupy in MSK had a view looking directly back across the busy York Avenue at the sprawling skyscraper of NYP. I remember laughing with Netu as he wheeled me through the car park, past the yellow taxis on York Avenue and into the front door of MSK. It felt like a scene out of *One Flew Over the Cuckoo's Nest*. This is weird I thought, but I knew it was not a dream.

In what had already been a very surreal morning, Netu then intercepted Ruth and the three children somewhere on York Avenue. The three children would go for the rest of the day with *his* nanny. It was all sorted. He then escorted Ruth to where she would spend most of the next 52 days with me, and make some of the most difficult decisions of her life. Ruth is very strong and very pragmatic, but I knew when she came into the room that *I* had still not yet realised the significance of my diagnosis. The 'rescue mission' and dash across York Avenue may have provided some temporary amusement but I was becoming increasingly aware there was no longer anything to laugh about. We spent the next hour with Dr Jurcic (head of haematology at MSK and whose confidence-inspiring care throughout was incredible) and the amazing Elizabeth, Dr Jurcic's nurse specialist. I don't remember any of the conversation that day except the bit where Ruth and I laughed when they asked us about sperm donation!

In fact I don't remember much of the next two weeks. I had a serious bacterial and fungal pneumonia. They couldn't give me any chemotherapy because of the infection and I only learned later that Ruth had to have several difficult discussions with the team during those weeks as to whether to delay chemo because of the risks of the infection or to go ahead and give it because of the risks of the leukaemia. Either way death was a very likely outcome. I was too 'morphined-up' to make any meaningful contribution or even to know about the discussions taking place.

I do however recall the week after the bone marrow biopsy. The Attending came in and told us the full results. It was definitely acute lymphoblastic leukaemia, and it was Philadelphia-chromosome positive. I remembered little about leukaemia from my student days but did remember there were 'bad ones' and 'worse ones', and this was one of the 'worse ones'. In fact, I scored badly in just about every negative prognostic marker there was. Ruth cried that day. It was the first time I had seen her cry since diagnosis and I then realised things were very bad.

STARTING CHEMOTHERAPY

Ruth's mum had arrived in Manhattan the day after I was diagnosed. She became the sixth member of the family unit, and accordingly Ruth's dad became the most frequent face on our Skype account! Children weren't allowed into the haematology ward for infection reasons so Ruth's mum selflessly looked after all three children during the day, thereby allowing Ruth to spend the time at the hospital with me. Not being able to see the children was one of the hardest aspects of being in hospital.

Despite the infection the decision was made to start chemotherapy. I don't remember recovering from the infection before the side effects of the chemotherapy started but I do remember the words of Dr Jurcic: 'This will be very difficult but our intention is cure and nothing short of it'.

I became a medical text book of chemotherapy side effects. Without embellishing or exaggerating I encountered just about everything that could be thrown my way. I had already scored badly in the things that might make my leukaemia more curable, I was on four different antibiotics to fight the infection, and now the chemo completely wiped me out. This isn't a diatribe on chemotherapy side effects but nausea, vomiting and complete anorexia were for me by far the worst. I have no practical or medical advice on how to cope with it. I didn't. But eventually it just went away.

The two other things I found very difficult, both at the time of my initial treatment and after being allowed back home, were more surprising. Several years earlier when Ruth and I had travelled round the Antipodes I completely shaved my hair off (or at least Ruth did under permission and strict supervision!) I knew it wasn't a good look for me but it was fun and given we wouldn't see anyone we knew for weeks it didn't matter. When my hair fell out after chemo I felt completely different. I'm not overly vain but the dramatic change in my appearance shocked and upset me. It coincided with me losing over 30 kg (five stone) in less than six weeks, which didn't help. When I looked at myself in the mirror I looked like an alien. I saw what I perceived as a skeletal, bald, cancer patient. It wasn't me. It was as though I was looking at someone else.

Secondly the tiredness, complete loss of energy and loss of any ability to concentrate I found frustrating. It wasn't relieved by sleep and all I could do for weeks was just lie there. I lived in a strange 'middle earth' somewhere between sleep and wakefulness. I had always told Ruth that if I ever got sick I didn't want or need any one sitting round the bedside on a prolonged basis. But when this happened I loved having Ruth at my bedside for virtually the whole time. I hated it when she left at night to go back home. Selfishly I always asked her to stay as long as possible, even until I had fallen asleep, forgetting that she would have to walk home alone and in the dark. She never said no.

PROBLEMS, PREDNISOLONE, AND THE PLANE HOME

During my initial treatment in MSK I was in hospital for a total of 52 days and the bill was almost $600,000. Yes, that is the correct number of zeros! Thankfully it was all covered by the health insurance that I had arranged through my employers (MSK!) on the day I started work. When I was diagnosed with leukaemia, Dr Rusch, the Head of Thoracic Surgery, ensured the continuation of my salary, our apartment, and my health insurance. I was treated like a VIP and no one could have done more to help us.

However, there was no official sick pay entitlement for temporary staff at MSK. Everything was connected and 'officially' if your salary stopped, you also lost your health insurance and your accommodation. Unknown to us, it was only through the 'persuasion' of many prominent physicians within the hospital and their relationship with the powers-that-be that my salary (and therefore everything else) had continued when I became sick. This would have significant implications for us at a later time, when we least expected it.

As a result of the genetics of my leukaemia (Philadelphia chromosome) I would need a bone marrow transplant after my initial chemotherapy. Returning to the UK after the induction chemo to have the transplant was a possible option but after much discussion with the haematology team Ruth and I decided to stay in New York. But I needed a donor. Although

I never really considered the possibility of not getting a donor, there are many leukaemia patients who don't get a suitable match or who only find one when it's too late.

The best donor is usually a sibling as this reduces the risk of the transplant fighting the recipient – so called Graft versus Host disease. Both my brothers came out to New York and while they were there gave a blood sample to check if their genetics would match. They were a perfect match...for each other! But completely incompatible with me. My cousin in Toronto (Kevin's older brother) gave blood but he didn't match either. The transplant team would need to find an unrelated donor and from then on I would (affectionately I'm sure!) be referred to as a 'MUD' (matched unrelated donor).

I initially struggled greatly with the timing of my diagnosis. I could almost accept the leukaemia, but had it happened six months earlier when we were still settled in Cambridge and with a supportive church family it would surely have removed many additional concerns and fears, particularly for Ruth. Alternatively had I been diagnosed six months later I may have been settled in a consultant job with the stability that would have provided. Additionally, we had even seen our financial advisor immediately prior to going to the US who suggested we enjoy our time out there and we could sort the finances on my return. For 99,999 out of 100,000 healthy 33-year-olds that is usually good advice. For me it turned out not to be.

However, after the initial trauma of what had happened, where it had happened, and when it had happened, Ruth and I actually began to believe that perhaps we had been in New York precisely because of the leukaemia, that there was in fact divine purpose in the timing. Memorial Sloan-Kettering is one of the biggest and best cancer hospitals in the world. They had a massive haematology department. Their bone marrow transplant team (separate to the leukaemia team) was also huge with over ten transplants being carried out *per week*! Surely God had directed us there to receive the best medical care available?

As described, the initial chemotherapy was very tough but I survived and was discharged back to the apartment. The proximity of our accommodation allowed me to be seen in clinic everyday. A donor was also found and the transplant was scheduled for January 2008. We would now be there for at least one year. We felt very comfortable with our decision to remain in the States for all the aforementioned reasons. In addition, all the MSK staff were incredible.

My appetite improved, my strength slowly increased and I even started venturing back out into the Upper East Side. I went back to church and was privileged to hear Tim Keller preach on several occasions. My excursions even included a trip to the cinema, for which I was advised to wear a fetching face mask to reduce the risk of infection. Thankfully in New York nothing is considered particularly abnormal but I fear wearing the same mask in downtown Belfast may have evoked a slightly different response! Aside from style the other great disadvantage of the mask was it greatly limited the speed of popcorn consumption. Sharing a box with my brother turned out to be a very bad move!

It came completely out of the blue when Ruth received the 'heads up' phone call from Dr Rusch. My thoracic boss was one of the most eminent thoracic surgeons in the world. I had worked for her for three months before getting sick and found her to be one of the most inspiring people ever to work for in any sphere of life. When I became unwell she became for Ruth and me a wise and comforting friend who wielded significant power within MSK. Her phone call to Ruth was to let us know unofficially that a management meeting had reviewed our case and could no longer perpetuate a salary (and therefore apartment and health insurance) for someone who was essentially doing no work for the hospital. My case became famous throughout the hospital but despite the protestations of the physicians (including Drs Rusch and Jurcic), a petition to management from dozens of members of staff, and even the offer of several staff to give up their annual leave to fund my salary (considering a consultant surgeon receives two weeks' annual leave per year this offer completely blew us away) the decision was unlikely to be revoked. Dr Rusch advised Ruth that on the basis of this information we needed to prepare ourselves for the outcome – we would have to return to the UK, as soon as possible. MSK would not continue our care.

Why now? We were completely resolved and content with our decision to stay in the US for another year. A donor had been found and we were confident of God's guiding hand in leading us to the right place at the right time. This phone call seemed to shatter that comfort. Looking rationally at the situation the decision was completely understandable.

My case was completely unprecedented and MSK had appropriately strict regulations concerning temporary staff. In the heat of the moment however, few of us are ever fully rational. Looking back, and even at the time, I have nothing but immense praise for all the staff I ever encountered in one of the best hospitals I have ever worked in.

We probably would have dwelt longer on the 'why is this happening now?' had we not immediately had to make a very difficult decision – where would we go back to in the UK? There were three obvious choices: London, Cambridge or Belfast. MSK had good links with London but from a family point of view it would have been a disaster. Cambridge was our home; we still had a house there and a great church. But we had been told of the need for as much family support as possible following the transplant and we had no direct family living in or around Cambridge. As a doctor 'big numbers' (as a surrogate of their experience of transplants) and reputation impressed me. But perhaps as a result of having to leave New York I became very convinced that God's plan for my treatment and subsequent remission, cure or otherwise, would not be changed by the hospital where I received my treatment. There are many things that I have coped with badly since diagnosis, but after the initial shock of being told finance had been withdrawn, we both accepted that we were going back to the UK.

Ultimately we decided to go back to Northern Ireland. We both had lots of family and friends there but there was one major problem – Belfast haematology unit could not do the sort of transplant that I needed (the MUD). So although I would initially (and subsequently) be under the Belfast team, the transplant would take place in Dublin, 100 miles from where we would live, and a three hour car journey away.

As we were in the process of deciding where we should go back to in the UK, I was receiving outpatient 'maintenance' treatment in the form of steroids and a chemotherapy agent called vincristine. After the first dose of vincristine I suffered a well known but serious complication – bowel ileus. Essentially, secondary to a complicated neuropathy, the bowels decide not to work at all and distend causing extreme abdominal pain. I was readmitted from clinic to MSK and although the staff were great as usual, there was no specific treatment to solve the problem swiftly. It was a huge blow to be readmitted, especially as I had been doing well since discharge. The treatments that were given to ease the problem were decidedly undignified but the worst problem was not being allowed to eat or drink anything – so called 'nil by mouth'. I was on steroids that had shot my appetite up through the roof, but nothing was allowed to pass my lips. The steroids also wrecked sleeping patterns and I remember two consecutive days and nights without any sleep at all. The only thing that cheered me at all was when, about 3am, I found the film *Gladiator* on one of the channels and was able to lose myself for a while and imagine I was instead a war hero who defeated all the bad guys! Generally it was dreadful and those two weeks of readmission were two of the worst weeks of the last two and a half years; mentally, physically and spiritually.

Despite my difficult abdominal problem, the leukaemia side of things was okay. The induction treatment had put me into remission and the aim of the maintenance treatment, of which the steroids and vincristine were a part, was to continue that remission until the transplant. Knowing the ileus had significantly interrupted the maintenance treatment and that we had to go back to the UK as soon as possible or we would soon be charged for our care, Ruth and I consulted with Dr Jurcic (who was amazing the whole way through) as to when we could go back. He was slightly taken aback and suggested waiting for several weeks. At this stage I was still an inpatient with a potentially life-threatening ileus ('mega-colon') and so his time frame was appropriate. But now we just wanted home. He did acknowledge that there was some degree of urgency to return to the UK as, including the search for another donor, the transplant still needed to be set up back in Dublin.

As soon as my bowels started showing signs of improvement, Ruth and I booked our flights home from the internet in my hospital room. Within days of our conversation with Dr Jurcic all five of us, a great friend from home who had come out specifically to help fly me home, my dad and I were all on the way to JFK airport to return to Northern Ireland. I was very sad leaving. This wasn't the way New York was supposed to end. In the airport we hired a wheelchair and I do remember laughing as I was wheeled through the airport terminal. We were allowed to bypass all the queues at security. We slipped into the executive lounge and never looked back. It again felt like a scene out of *One Flew Over the Cuckoo's Nest*. This is weird I thought, but I knew it was not a dream. I was going home.

*For I know that my Redeemer lives, and at the last he will
stand upon the earth. And after my skin has been thus
destroyed, yet in my flesh I shall see God, whom I shall see
for myself, and my eyes shall behold, and not another*

JOB 19:25-27

I n the first section on chapters 1 and 2 of Job we saw his seemingly
unmerited and undeserved suffering. He was a good man who had
everything taken away from him; his possessions, all his children, and
finally his health as well. We saw that while God permitted Satan limited
power, it was only to accomplish the opposite of what Satan had intended.
We saw that God is totally sovereign in everything and that although God
may not specifically have planned our particular suffering, by the time it
reaches us, it has completely got his permission.

We reviewed why God allows suffering and saw that what *he* wants for
us may be different from what *we* think is good for us, because he is God
and we are not. Finally we saw how the book of Job points to Jesus who
underwent the ultimate unjust, undeserved, unmerited human suffering.
We don't always get a reason 'why' to explain each experience of pain and
each episode of suffering, but we are provided with a 'who' to help us
face our suffering with hope rather than bitterness, to give us courage
rather than despair. We have Jesus with us rather than being alone,
because he has been there before us.

But why does this book not now jump from chapter 2 to chapter 42? Job
had resisted cursing God. God had won. Why not jump to Job's glorious

restoration at the end of 42 when 'the Lord blessed the latter days of Job more than his beginning' (v12)? It would certainly save a lot of reading. In our 'Read the Bible in a Year' diary it would get us off to a cracking start, wouldn't it? If we just missed out most of Job!

But if we did that, we would be missing out on something huge, something authentic, something real, because we must understand there is a significant difference between acute and chronic suffering. How we respond initially to tragedy or disaster or suffering when it first strikes, when the policeman arrives at the door, when the phone call we dread finally arrives, when the doctor gives us the positive biopsy result, when the employer gives us the bottom line, can be very different from our response when the suffering or the pain or the grief takes root and stays with us for days or weeks or months. When it doesn't go away. When it doesn't all get better.

In the adrenaline-soaked drama of an emergency, humans can do amazing things. We all know powerful stories of bravery and courage from the frontlines of war, from car accidents and natural disasters. But when the dust has settled, the adrenaline has gone and the reality sinks in, those wonderful acts of humanity seem a distant past as the memories become the nightmares.

Similarly, when initially told of our suffering we sometimes respond so well. We can say confidently 'the Lord gives and the Lord has taken away'. We can even say 'blessed be the name of the Lord'. We comfort ourselves (and are initially comforted by well-meaning others) with platitudes and well quoted Bible verses. But then later, with the loneliness of the empty house, the reality of lost dreams, the chronicity of our pain, the constant reminder of the picture on the mantelpiece, or the scars that no one else can see, we collapse in bitterness, resentment and confusion. Despite our faith, or perhaps because of it, we question God's seemingly hard hand upon our lives. Can you relate to that?

I share this not to sensationalise but to emphasise that at the start, when I received the diagnosis, I wasn't devastated, I wasn't angry, and I didn't ask: what in the world is going on? Perhaps blurred by morphine or just blunted by the shock it did not really hit me until a long time after the diagnosis was made. But as the weeks and months went by things became much tougher. As the side effects of treatment took their toll

I lost my hair and a third of my body weight, and more than a third of my strength. I saw the suffering of my wife and the confusion of my children, wondering why daddy couldn't play or even get out of bed. I saw consultant jobs being advertised that should have been mine and I saw my friends and their families appearing to be able to carry on with their own lives as normal. I appreciate that many of them didn't carry on 'as normal', and were greatly affected by what was happening to Ruth and me, but as the months went on the reality of living out my faith during my suffering became much, much harder.

And so we come to Job's incredible faith. Despite losing his wealth and his family he so far was not rewarded with healing. Remember the longevity of his suffering: 'so I am allotted months of emptiness, and nights of misery are apportioned to me' (7:3). Job's misery was not going away. He may well have asked: 'Why, since I resisted the initial temptation to curse God, and I have continued to worship God despite my suffering, have I not been restored or healed?' But had Job been healed immediately, had this book jumped to chapter 42 or ended at chapter 2, it would be inauthentic and unreal. It is precisely because Job, now dealing with his chronic suffering and his long term struggles, behaves in such a normal human way, that his story can be so helpful to us.

In this chapter I want us to move with Job through his own arguments and his continued experience of suffering. I want us to see how Job copes (or doesn't cope) by looking at his faith in three ways: the defence of his faith, the hope of his faith, and the wisdom of his faith.

THE DEFENCE OF JOB'S FAITH (CHAPTER 2:11 - CHAPTER 25)

Now when Job's three friends heard of all this evil that had come upon him, they came each from his own place, Eliphaz the Temanite, Bildad the Shuhite, and Zophar the Naamathite. They made an appointment together to come to show him sympathy and comfort him. And when they saw him from a distance, they did not recognise him. And they raised their voices and wept, and they tore their robes and sprinkled dust on their heads toward heaven. And they sat with him on the ground seven days and seven nights, and no one spoke a word to him, for they saw that his suffering was very great. (2:11-13)

Many say his friends initially got it so right in their silence. Often we are too hard on them. They had come a long way. They had come because they cared. They came and seeing how utterly grief-stricken he was they sat with him on the ground, wept with him, and said nothing.

But their silence may have been less helpful than we often assume. The Bible suggests, albeit subtly, that their outward display of grief (the torn clothes, the dust on their heads) is actually what someone does when they are mourning with a corpse, not a friend who is still alive! They considered Job as good as dead and therefore simply had nothing to say, rather than displaying a sympathetic silence as we so often interpret it.

To a greater or lesser degree, those who suffer will do so alone and in fact in chapter 3:1 it was Job, not his friends, who eventually broke the silence. 'After this Job opened his mouth and cursed the day of his birth.' He complains that now he can't die, even though he longs for it: 'Why is light given to him who is in misery, and life to the bitter in soul, who long for death, but it comes not, and dig for it more than for hidden treasures, who rejoice exceedingly and are glad when they find the grave?' (3:20-22)

Job so wanted to come through this ordeal without denying his God, but he was beginning to think that the only way *he* could see that happening was for God to crush him before he was crushed by his own suffering. Interestingly, in our secular world with increasing sympathy towards 'assisted death' and 'dignity in dying', any thoughts of Job ending his own life seem far from his mind. His life belongs to God and it is only God who can take it.

We can certainly draw our principles regarding suicide or assisted suicide from a biblical perspective, but I believe the biblical examples cannot be used *per se* to extrapolate a general Christian ethic towards suicide and I have no intention of doing so here. The reason I mention this at all however, is that several people have asked me since my diagnosis if suicide is ever something I considered. I can honestly say it is not. For most of the last two and a half years, cure was a medical possibility. But even after relapse, when medically speaking cure was no longer an option, thoughts of suicide never even crossed my mind.

However, we should also recognise that despair even to the point of considering suicide was something experienced by a number of other biblical figures, who are clearly presented in a favourable light. One thinks immediately of Paul, David, Jeremiah and Elijah. The great hymn writer William Cowper suffered severe depression and considered suicide several times. This does not mean they ever had any intention of 'going through with it', but it should alert us to be cautious in condemning the Christian who experiences despair or suicidal thoughts. Suicidal thinking is an authentic Christian experience but we should remember that while God does not test us further than we are able to bear (1 Corinthians 10:13) we are able to bear considerably more than we care to think.

For those who are able then to survive such an experience and to retain faith, however weak, it is a glorious witness and a glorious testimony to God's faithfulness – exemplified by Job. But I firmly believe the right to life is a unilateral contract between God and man, and is therefore non-negotiable. As ordinary human beings we don't have this prerogative.

Job's friends, Eliphaz, Zophar and Bildad, had perhaps been sympathetic initially, or perhaps just had nothing to say, thinking Job was as good as dead. But then they can't hold back and like a burst dam spend the next three cycles of dialogue from chapters 3-25 pummelling Job. They repeatedly spell out a principle of justice that they so wrongly and inappropriately apply to Job: 'who that was innocent ever perished?' (4:7). Trouble comes to those who sin and the innocent do not perish. If you're suffering Job, you must have done something wrong.

'As I have seen, those who plough iniquity and sow trouble reap the same. By the breath of God they perish, and by the blast of his anger they are consumed' (4:8-9). Eliphaz is totally convinced that beneath the godly, pious veneer of Job lurks some deep sinful past or present. He is a pervert, a fraud, a murderer. To him and the other friends, suffering is the result of wickedness, and prosperity is the result of righteousness. Joe Bayly, speaking about the death of his children says, 'someone came to visit me, he talked incessantly about God's dealings, of why it happened, about hope beyond the grave, about things I knew were true. I was unmoved except to wish he'd go away. Another came and sat beside me. He didn't speak. He just sat and listened. When I said something he answered briefly, prayed simply. He left. I was moved. I was comforted. I hated to see him go.' [10]

---

10. Joseph Bayly. *The view from a hearse. A Christian view of death*. DC Cook Publishing company, 1973. p40

Personally speaking, from the day I was diagnosed with leukaemia to the present, my wife Ruth and I have experienced many different attitudes and approaches to our situation. I do not doubt in any way that all meant well as texts, calls, letters, emails, cards, prayers, and people have come to us from all over the world and by every delivery route available. So many family, close friends, and other people we had never even heard of have selflessly and persistently continued to meet our needs in whatever way they can. One close friend emailed or texted me every single night for well over a year, always with a word of encouragement and inspiration about God's continued presence and love. This humbled us beyond imagination and most will never fully know how much it meant to us.

However, as an example of how to do spiritual and pastoral care we have been overwhelmed by the approach of our pastor and friend from Cambridge. Steve came to visit us many times in New York, Belfast, Dublin, Broughshane and in God's grace in Cambridge too. When he came, to echo the words of Joe Bayly, many times 'he didn't speak. He just sat and listened. When I said something he answered briefly, prayed simply. He left. I was moved. I was comforted. I hated to see him go.' Steve, however, also knew the timing of how and when to introduce God's word to our situation. Without platitudes or empty promises of physical healing in this life, he lovingly and graciously redirected us to God's word, the promises that were there, and the challenges that still remained despite our thinking things couldn't get any worse.

I remember one particular occasion when he laid down the challenge of how I could continue to be used for God's purposes *in* my current situation, not when it was all potentially better. When I had my ileus and was not allowed to eat or drink Steve realised that without meals my day lacked any structure. So he came every morning and instead of breakfast we just read the Bible together, working through a section of *Explore* notes. Steve's patience and 'intentional' ministry helped Ruth and I through many hard times and we will be forever grateful for his love, guidance and support.

The friends of Job, however, just got frustrated with him. They got impatient. They wanted to impose their opinion, perhaps neatly wrapped in biblical jargon. But they just didn't have the patience that was needed to help him through his suffering. Job's sarcasm in chapter 12:2 (paraphrased) is a reflection of how their theology is affecting Job:

'Oh, yes, you are so wise…when you die I am really worried that there won't be any wise people left in the world'.

How much patience do we have when working through our own or someone else's suffering or problems? Do we want the quick-fix or are we prepared to be shaped by God's timing? When our friend is suffering can we just sit and listen, however long that may take, however long that may go on for? Or are we desperate to jump in with our own opinion, our own explanation of why something is happening, and our own theology of suffering, albeit neatly wrapped in biblical jargon? When people come to us with their struggles and with their suffering do we initially take the time and have the patience just to listen?

And so in the defence of Job's faith we see first that Job's friends might have had correct theology, but it was wrongly applied. Job's comforters sound reasonable most of the time. It's mostly okay, at least if not taken out of context. It would be much easier to dispense with if what Job's friends say was complete nonsense. That would make things much easier. But much of it would have us making notes in the margin if we heard it at a conference!

The Bible does say that ultimately the righteous will prosper and the evil will suffer. Aren't the Proverbs and the Psalms full of that sort of stuff? Suffering is a reflection of human sin, and the uglier the suffering the uglier and more grotesque the sin. If we knew Job had sinned then there would be some rationale in assuming God was disciplining his servant (Proverbs 3:11-12). But we are told at the start that Job was blameless. This doesn't infer he was sinless, but it certainly is enough for us to assume it was not because of any sin he had committed that Job was being allowed to suffer.

Suffering can be a direct result of something we do that is wrong. More often, however, it reflects the corporate sin of humanity and cannot be interpreted always to reflect the specific sin of the individual. So there is some truth in what the friends say, yet Job's friends were trying to kill him with so many true statements wrongly, insensitively, unlovingly, and superficially applied. 'Good' or 'correct' theology that is applied superficially, insensitively and incorrectly, then becomes 'bad' theology and can be devastating for those who hear it. Be careful what you say either to yourself in your time of suffering or to someone else in theirs.

That said, we must also be aware that there are consequences of our sin. We may be suffering as a direct consequence of something we have done. But suffering and prosperity are not distributed in the world in proportion to the evil or good that we do. Job is right. The worst people often seem to do okay, while the just and blameless become a laughing stock. The best may suffer the most, and the worst may look okay. But the friends relied on human reason more than biblical wisdom and in that they were wrong. Holding on to what he knows is true, Job is thus able to resist the false theology of his friends and resist their accusations: 'worthless physicians are you all' (13:4).

Secondly, in the defence of his faith Job still seeks God. Job protests his innocence: 'for I have not denied the words of the Holy One' (6:10). The friends' line of argument doesn't cut it with Job and so he demands an answer from the very top: 'But I would speak to the Almighty, and I desire to argue my case with God' (13:3).

Reading through these chapters reveals Job pouring out his soul. When things are down we cannot hide our innermost feelings from God: 'I am feeble and crushed; I groan because of the tumult of my heart. O Lord, all my longing is before you; my sighing is not hidden from you' (Psalm 38:8-9).

Our feelings will at times be incongruent with our faith – as were Job's, but sometimes it is only by verbalising our deepest feelings that we realise how wrong or skewed they are, and so openness and honesty in our prayers are essential. Mark Ashton comments that the book of Job is not primarily a book about suffering or even about sovereignty but about prayer. It is full of Job's prayers, pleading his case, defending his case, being honest and open before his creator God. But despite his desire to talk with God we come to chapter 23 and Job still hears nothing, just screaming empty silence, like the door being slammed in his face and the sound of the bolts going across on the other side:

Oh, that I knew where I might find him, that I might come even to his seat! I would lay my case before him and fill my mouth with arguments. I would know what he would answer me and understand what he would say to me. Would he contend with me in the greatness of his power? No; he would pay attention to me. There an upright man could argue with him, and I would be acquitted forever by my judge. Behold, I go forward, but he is not there, and backward, but I do not perceive him; on the left hand when he is working, I do not behold him; he turns to the right hand, but I do not see him. (23:3-9)

Do you know what that feels like in your suffering? No answer from God. Job has bared his soul to the Lord, opened up his aching heart, his darkness, and his despair. He has been honest, even offensive in his prayers, but God seems to have shut the door and just walked away.

Yet despite his incorrect assumptions that God is not there, God is actually working in Job and slowly correcting his thinking. Similarly, if we are honest and open with God then he will correct our thinking as well and we will see that he is still there: 'When you pass through the waters I will be with you; and through the rivers, they shall not overwhelm you; when you walk through fire you shall not be burned and the flame shall not consume you. For I am the Lord your God, the Holy One of Israel, your Saviour.' (Isaiah 43:2-3). God will not let you do this thing alone. He will always be there.

Consider too Jesus' own openness and honesty in prayer as he cried out in the Garden of Gethsemane: 'please Lord, if there is any other way, take this cup away from me so that I don't have to drink the cup of your wrath'. On the cross Jesus cried 'My God, why have you forsaken me? Why Lord? Why?'

Job feels crushed by God's sovereignty. Job feels that God does not even hear his cries. We too may at times feel crushed by God's sovereignty but we must be assured that we have a mediator who has been there first before us. We have a Saviour, Jesus, who has not only cried out for us, who understands our pain, and who hears our cries, but who has actually been there for us. In Hebrews chapter 2 we have God himself, leaving the royalty and the grandeur of his throne in heaven to become 'lower than the angels' (Hebrews 2:9), to become human (2:14), to become one of us. But Jesus did not even go from being God to becoming perhaps a ruling king or a president, but he emptied himself of everything by taking on the form and nature of a slave, by looking just like other men, and by sharing in human nature.

Jesus, though he is fully God, became fully man in order that we might be fully saved. He did so in order that he could die on our behalf and identify with us in everything, and especially in our suffering: 'For we do not have a high priest who is unable to sympathise with our weaknesses, but one who in every respect has been tempted as we are, yet without sin. Let us then with confidence draw near to the throne of grace, that we may receive mercy and find grace to help in time of need.' (Hebrews 4:15-16).

In your suffering are you still seeking God? Do we still cry out to the one who does hear us and who does hold us? Despite what it may feel like, do we hold onto God because we know that he is still there?

THE HOPE OF JOB'S FAITH (CHAPTER 19)

If all Job's friend's can do is smear his character, if all they can do is criticise him and accuse him of self-indulgence, then why don't they just shut up and at least let him argue his case with God? They have reduced faith, hope and love to moralism and lectures. But Job has something else to say:

Behold, my eye has seen all this, my ear has heard and understood it. What you know, I also know; I am not inferior to you. But I would speak to the Almighty, and I desire to argue my case with God. As for you, you whitewash with lies; worthless physicians are you all. Oh that you would keep silent, and it would be your wisdom! Hear now my argument and listen to the pleadings of my lips. (13:1-6)

Despite his accusations about God and at God, Job actually deep down still longs for God's presence. He longs for God to speak and has said he wants an audience with the Almighty. But despite the seemingly endless repetition of argument with his friends, something has been happening to Job and while his thinking is by no means clear, or his questions fully answered, when we reach chapter 19 Job bursts into an eruption of faith. Christopher Ash comments that in Handel's *Messiah* there is a famous soprano aria in which Handel puts Job 19:25-26 alongside 1 Corinthians 15:20:

I know that my Redeemer lives
          and at the last he will stand upon the earth.
And after my skin has been thus destroyed
          yet in my flesh I shall see God.
For now is Christ risen from the dead,
          the first-fruits of them that sleep.

Though he didn't fully know it, Job's confidence was not wishful thinking, because we can look at his hope that 'My Redeemer lives' and say with assurance that Christ has risen from the dead. The omnipotent, all-loving God did once attack someone with the full force of his power, someone who was perfect and 'blameless', but someone who was raised to life on the third day thereby vindicating himself and all who would follow after him. So Job's hope is not in vain. As he relentlessly battles back, attacks and exposes the theology of his friends for what it is, something is clarifying itself in Job:

For I know that my Redeemer lives, and at the last he will stand upon the earth. And after my skin has been thus destroyed, [the skin that is infected and sore and crawling with worms, the disease that makes me an object of ridicule and contempt] *yet in my flesh I shall see God, whom I shall see for myself, and my eyes shall behold, and not another. My heart faints within me!'* (19: 25-27)

Some may still debate the reality of the resurrection but in our postmodern society more and more people are becoming less and less concerned with whether the resurrection happened or not. The issue is not so much whether the resurrection did or didn't happen…but what's it got to do with them? How does it affect me? What is the relevance to me?

In John 20:10-14 when Mary finds the empty tomb and thinks it's all a disaster one commentator writes: 'Just like other sorrowing disciples since, Mary doesn't realise that in her grief, when she thought life couldn't possibly get any worse… she actually has angels in front of her and her Lord behind her.'[11] John 20 teaches us that because the resurrection happened, you may not fully understand what is going on but there are angels in front of us and Jesus behind us. Here's Mary, and all around her is the greatest act of love and of power that God has ever performed. Here's Mary, about to become one of the most famous people in the world, and she is thinking it's all a disaster. What good could possibly come from this? Not only has her Lord been killed, but now his body has been stolen as well!

Maybe you are looking around at all the things going wrong in your life, and thinking 'I can't see what God could possibly be doing here, and even

---

11. Quoted by Tim Keller, London Men's Convention 2009, Talk 2: *The Resurrection*, available at *http://sthelens.audiop.org.uk*. Source of quotation unknown.

though I pray I don't feel Jesus is near'...but guess what? If the resurrection happened, then even though you don't feel it, don't see it, aren't aware of Jesus being near you...you are wrong. When you think life couldn't get any worse, if you clear the tears, and peer through the dimness...there are angels in front of you and Jesus behind you - your Redeemer lives!

The great heavyweight boxing champion Muhammad Ali once said of religion: 'I don't want no pie in the sky when I die; I want something real here on the ground while I'm still around'. Job realises that while there will be times when it will seem that everything around us is just one big fog, it is a fog tinged with clarity. And it's those moments of clarity that help us navigate through the fog.

For some of us our religion is purely a matter of duty. We've gone to church, even been raised as a Christian, but it has failed to change our lives and our priorities. Maybe we are a slave to achievement, or position or status, or to family, or moral superiority...but salvation, because it is achieved and received by weakness - Jesus' death and resurrection - pulls off a complete reversal of the values of this world with regard to power, recognition, status and wealth. What if we were a community filled with a reversal of values, where our hopes were based solidly and solely in the power of the resurrection? How would we look to our friends? How would we look to our colleagues and our community?

Job shows the resurrection is relevant because when we think the bottom has fallen out of our world, to use the John 20 analogy, we just need to open our eyes and we will see that we have angels in front of us and Jesus standing right behind us - see that 'my Redeemer lives'. The resurrection is relevant because if we think we do not deserve God's grace, even in the resurrection, Jesus affirms that salvation is for everyone, regardless of pedigree, merit or class. The resurrection is relevant because Job is finally sure that even if his suffering takes him all the way to death itself, as might well have been the case for him (remember he couldn't see chapter 42 and didn't know whether he was going to live or die, as might be the case for you too), yet he is sure that even in death he will meet his God as his Redeemer and not as an angry judge. He will be redeemed from his misery. His body will be renewed. His sickness will be gone.

People sometimes ask me how I cope, knowing I've probably only got months to live. The answer is very simple. Like Job I believe in the resurrection. Therefore I believe the Bible when it says 'For I consider that the sufferings of this present time are not worth comparing with the glory that is to be revealed to us' (Romans 8:18). I believe the Bible when Jesus says 'I am the resurrection and the life. Whoever believes in me, though he die, yet shall he live, and everyone who lives and believes in me shall never die' (John 11:25-26). I believe the Bible when it promises 'knowing that he who raised the Lord Jesus will raise us also with Jesus and bring us with you into his presence' (2 Corinthians 4:14).

Many will argue that if your religion excites you, if it fulfils you, if it's 'good for you', then great, go for it. But Christianity says the opposite. Christianity says don't believe in it because it's encouraging (though it is), don't believe in it because it's moving (though it is), don't even believe in it because it offers hope (though it does); believe in it because it's true, because the resurrection really happened.

While this confidence does not totally solve Job's problems, it does enable him to be sure that God does know where he is: 'But he knows the way that I take; when he has tried me, I shall come out as gold' (Job 23:10). Job feels he is clinging on by his fingers but deep down knows that even if he lets go he will not fall. Job hasn't turned from God, but more importantly he knows that God hasn't turned from him. God isn't absent. Be assured in your suffering that God isn't absent. He knows exactly where you are. He knows what you are going through and if you do follow the Jesus of Calvary, he knows that when you have finished, when he has tested and tried you, even if it is on the other side of death itself, you too will 'come out as gold'. Meaninglessness makes the furnace unbearable, but faith says God knows what he is doing, even if that means death – 'yet in the resurrection, in our flesh we will see God, with our own eyes'.

Where is the hope of your faith? Where is your strength really based? Is it in the bank balance, the monthly salary, the inheritance left for the children, the security of your spouse or family circle? Is it in the doctors or the drugs that they give out? Is it in status or position or success? All these may provide some sort of superficial, short term appearance of security but they will all be taken from you. Having once had them and now having lost them might even be the source of your suffering.

Or is your hope and strength in what you know to be true about God? That when he has tested you, you will come forth as gold, that you will see him as your Redeemer and your Lord, with your own eyes? That though outwardly we are wasting away, yet inwardly we are being renewed day by day? For our light and momentary troubles are achieving for us an eternal glory that far outweighs them. So do we fix our eyes not on what is seen (the sickness, the death, the pain, the suffering; or even just on the wrinkles, the worsening vision or hearing or mobility, the slow decline that old age will not let us avoid) but on what is unseen, on Jesus and heaven and eternity? For what is seen is temporary, but what is unseen is eternal (see 2 Corinthians 4:16-18). Do we live our lives based on that, or are we really living just for the good things that help temporarily to palliate our pain?

But despite some clarification in Job's thinking, God still has good reason for not letting him alone until his refining is done. So we turn finally to look at what needs to be the wisdom of Job's faith.

THE WISDOM OF JOB'S FAITH
(CHAPTER 28)

Surely there is a mine for silver, and a place for gold that they refine. Iron is taken out of the earth, and copper is smelted from the ore. Man puts an end to darkness and searches out to the farthest limit the ore in gloom and deep darkness. He opens shafts in a valley away from where anyone lives; they are forgotten by travellers; they hang in the air, far away from mankind; they swing to and fro...

Man puts his hand to the flinty rock and overturns mountains by the roots. He cuts out channels in the rocks, and his eye sees every precious thing. He dams up the streams so that they do not trickle, and the thing that is hidden he brings out to light. But where shall wisdom be found? And where is the place of understanding? Man does not know its worth, and it is not found in the land of the living. The deep says, 'It is not in me,' and the sea says, 'It is not with me.' It cannot be bought for gold, and silver cannot be weighed as its price. It cannot be valued in the gold of Ophir, in precious onyx or sapphire. Gold and glass cannot equal it, nor can it be exchanged for jewels of fine gold...

From where, then, does wisdom come? And where is the place of understanding? It is hidden from the eyes of all living and concealed from the birds of the air...

God understands the way to it, and he knows its place. For he looks to the
ends of the earth and sees everything under the heavens. When he gave
to the wind its weight and apportioned the waters by measure, when he
made a decree for the rain and a way for the lightning of the thunder,
then he saw it and declared it; he established it, and searched it out.
And he said to man, 'Behold, the fear of the Lord, that is wisdom, and
to turn away from evil is understanding.' (28:1-4, 9-17, 20-21, 23-28)

I make no apology for having this chapter of Job almost in full. Most
preachers would take an entire sermon (or more!) to tackle it by itself. But
if you take nothing away from this short book, please read and reread and
hold on to Job 28, and you will not go far wrong when suffering comes to
your door. It is not connected with the speeches of the three 'comforters',
nor is it directly connected with what is to follow. It's more like an
interlude or a reflective period on what has been, and perhaps on
what will come. The root of the problem of human suffering is partly
an over-estimation of us as regards our own wisdom and chapter
28 allows us to re-orientate the source of true wisdom.

Chapter 28 tells us that wisdom is a treasure that cannot be mined like iron
and copper (v2), that cannot be bought with gold and silver (v15). We can't
just go and pick it off the shelves at any supermarket. It's not even about
reading more books. It's far more than mere knowledge, because wisdom
is knowledge honed and refined by experience. It isn't about knowing the
answers to what God hasn't revealed – it's about living out our lives and
our faith in the light and the reality of what God has revealed!

When suffering comes to our door we spend (and waste) so much time
asking 'Why Lord? Why me? What in the world is going on?' So many
endless questions, so many of which will remain unanswered, at least
in this lifetime. But in the assurance that wisdom dwells with God alone
(v23) is where we must take refuge. Science and technology for all their
benefits won't tell you a thing about suffering. They might give you some
tablets to help ease the pain, but the source of true wisdom can only be
received if we listen to and submit before God our Creator. Why? Because
wisdom only comes from God (v28). Human reason is unreliable when
applied to the existence and nature of God.

You won't get a grip on suffering through human reason but you will get a
grip on it by experience and by listening to God through that experience.

What does this poem in chapter 28 say to Job and to us? It says that we must give up trying to solve Job's immense problems with 'bottom-up', human understanding. Human, earth-bound views won't get us the answer. Remember chapters 1 and 2? We won't find out what's going on by looking in the world and so the writer allows us that glimpse into heaven itself. We must address Job's suffering (and by application our suffering) with a top-down view, with the heavenly perspective we saw in chapters 1 and 2. John Stott writes that we have to learn to 'climb the hill called Calvary, and from that vantage-ground survey all life's tragedies. The cross doesn't solve the problem of suffering, but it supplies the essential perspective from which to look at it.'[12]

Recently my family were at Castlewellan Castle, a beautiful house and grounds in County Down, where they had great fun going round a large maze. The winner, or the first person to the middle, declared their victory by ringing a bell. Have you ever tried to go round a maze? Some are easy, but for a complicated one we may never get there if we stick to ground level. But if we get the opportunity to look from above how clear it all becomes. The right path, everything, can be seen right to its boundaries. The analogy is clear. Though in our suffering we rarely get to look from above we must trust the God who does, and know that he sees the path far more clearly than we do. This is wisdom.

Now I'm not suggesting that for each and every suffering a conversation takes place in heaven like chapters 1 and 2, but in our difficulties, suffering, struggles and pain we have to give up our endless wrestling and endless human debate and just allow the wisdom of the God of grace, his top-down wisdom, to hold us. Relief for Job is only found when he gives in and stops the questions and rests in what he knows of God's character: that God is sovereign; that God loves him and is still holding him in his hands.

The fear of the Lord (v28) is where our wisdom must begin. Fear of the Lord in the presence of suffering is the scary level unconditional trust, unconditional submission to God's sovereignty, to God's love, to the truth that God loves you in spite of how it looks. Remember Satan tried to prove Job was just in it for what he got out of it, but we must keep trusting God in the dark, trusting his love in the dark. It is the only

12. Quoted by Roger Steer. *Inside Story. The life of John Stott*. IVP, 2009, p219 from Stott, JS. *The Cross of Christ*. IVP, 20th Anniversary Edition, 2006

way we will become better rather than worse in our suffering. Behind the sovereignty of God there is a wisdom hidden from man (28:13). So let us be slow to judge God as capricious or cruel or foolish or out of control when we can't see God's wisdom in what he's doing. It may appear arbitrary, out of control, foolish to us; but when we don't have that top-down vantage point, the heavenly perspective, let us rest in knowing that God's wisdom is far greater than ours.

Perhaps verses 25-27 give us a hint of what God will ultimately say later on. But just as we can't give a four-year-old an explanation for everything that happens, for the reasons behind all our decisions, because they will not be consoled no matter what we say, because they are four and they won't understand, so God can't (because we wouldn't understand) and won't always give us an explanation, and so then we must just trust. And if we can do that, then despite the pain we will become wiser, humbler, and more sympathetic. Our faith and trust will be deepened and strengthened through our suffering rather than weakened and destroyed.

But because it would be impossible to hang on in the dark by abstract doctrine, CS Lewis says 'God wrote himself into the play'. God gave us Jesus. We must see Jesus being true to us in the dark – loving us despite his suffering, clinging on in Gethsemane and on the cross, holding on despite being abandoned by God. Jesus' death on the cross is the only time when God ever did the abandoning. And yet it is precisely because we can see Jesus being true to us in the dark that we know we will never be abandoned. John Stott again comments:

'I could never myself believe in God if it were not for the cross. The only God I believe in is the one Nietzsche ridiculed as 'God on the cross'. In the real world of pain, how could one worship a God who was immune to it? He laid aside his immunity to pain. He entered our world of flesh and blood, tears and death. He suffered for us. Our sufferings become more manageable in light of this.' [13]

Job has said enough. He rests his case: 'The words of Job are ended' (31:40). Job has now had enough of human reasoning, of logical explanation, of our bottom-up wisdom and I hope we have too. Now I believe God speaks with his wisdom rather than ours. We'll look at what

---

13. *Ibid*.

Elihu and God have to say in the next section. But chapter 36:15 (ultimately) reminds us that often for those who suffer God delivers them in their suffering, he delivers them in their afflictions, not from their suffering and afflictions. You may think God hasn't answered your prayers and hasn't heard you, but maybe he has. Maybe he is still speaking, just on a slightly different wavelength, on a different frequency that you haven't yet tuned into up until now. Perhaps, rather than remove your suffering, God is trying to speak to you in and through your suffering.

CONCLUSION

Experience is a brutal teacher. But we've seen through Job's experience how his faith has also now stood the test of time. In a defence of his faith he rejected the false theology of his friends: in this world suffering is not measured on how good or bad we are. We saw that the hope of his faith was based solely on the resurrection, and his knowledge that his Redeemer (and ours) lives, and that after death he would see God. Finally we have seen that the wisdom of Job's faith ultimately lay with God's wisdom, not man's; and with God's top-down view, not with human reasoning.

One of the key messages of Job is that the children of God, those who trust God, who are covered by Jesus' blood, who have called on him as their Saviour and Lord, who are being sanctified by his Spirit, still also *suffer*. But when they suffer God is still totally sovereign. Suffering is individually and expertly designed by the loving hand of our perfect physician, so that our faith might be refined, our holiness enlarged, and our God glorified.

Eliphaz asks in chapter 4:7: 'who that was innocent ever perished?' We can truly answer that question with only one name – Jesus. Don Carson, in his book *How long, O Lord?* writes: 'the truth of the matter is that all we have to do is live long enough and we will suffer...but in the darkest night of the soul, Christians have something to hold on to that Job could only imagine – we know a crucified Christ. We know that when there seems to be no other evidence of God's love, we cannot ever escape the cross. We know that when we suffer there will often be mystery, but we also know that if we look to Jesus and the cross rather than our suffering, there must also always be faith.'[14]

14. Carson DA. *How Long, O Lord?* (2nd edition): *Reflections on Suffering and Evil*. Baker Academic, 2006, p16

HOME

Home... I can't say where it is but I know I'm going there

U2

THE WORST CHRISTMAS EVER

Dublin airport was crowded. It was very close to Christmas and the entire world seemed to be coming to Ireland. At least that was the perspective I took when we arrived in the Dublin terminal. We hired a wheelchair but this time I didn't laugh. I quickly realised that coming 'home' was not the climax some people thought it would be.

We had loved New York; we had decided to stay there for the transplant. Being sent back had not totally sunk in. We both loved Northern Ireland and ultimately wanted to end up there. But not like this. For sure, there was a certain degree of relief and pleasure to be back with family and friends. I had been concerned for Ruth that if I had died in New York the amount of paperwork to 'get me back' would have been a nightmare. Knowing we would no longer even have to think about the financial side of our care was also a comfort (although the generosity of one particular relative both then and now was incredible and significantly alleviated many concerns in that regard). But Cambridge had been our home for the last ten years. Ruth and I and the children had never lived in Northern Ireland together. Our church, many close friends, and what had been our 'life' was very much based in Cambridge, not Northern Ireland. We still had a house in Cambridge that was full of all our stuff. Driving from Dublin to Belfast we were almost home, and yet at the same time we weren't.

Christmas Eve 2007 for me was one of the hardest nights in my whole illness. People called and kept telling us how wonderful it was we were back – and how happy we must be to be home. There was a large family party in the early evening but I stayed in a bedroom, in the dark and didn't appear down at all. Later on toys needed assembling for the next day. I had no strength or energy and couldn't even help put Josh's football posts together. I remember feeling so useless.

Christmas day came and went. The same Christmas dinner I had dreamed about when lying 'nil by mouth' in MSK looked great...but the ileus had not fully resolved so I could only eat in tiny portions. We protected the children as much as possible and superficially looked like we were having a good day. Inside I knew we weren't.

New Year, however, was a complete changing point for me. Ruth and I went to bed early on New Year's Eve, before Jools Holland's *Hootenanny* had even started. We prayed together as we have done every night since diagnosis, acknowledging God's sovereignty and praying for his healing and his help. We finally drifted off to sleep but I felt very sorry for myself. I felt sorry for Ruth. I felt sorry for the children. It should all have been so different.

But when I woke on New Year's Day something was different. I read the *Explore* notes for 1 January 2008. I can't remember what they were about but my attitude changed completely. There seemed to be some clarity amidst the fog and while nothing had changed physically, mentally I resolved no longer to feel quite as sorry for myself and to make the most of the situation for God, for Ruth, and for the children.

THE BONE MARROW TRANSPLANT

Marrow transplants are unpredictable and the minimum hospital stay is usually about 6-8 weeks. There is a high risk of complications and depending on the severity these can lead to months in hospital or even death. I was given a 25% risk of death at the time of the transplant. I used to tell patients that statistics apply to populations and are less helpful for individuals. Despite my confidence that God was in control, as a patient I held on to, ruminated on, and remembered all the stats that were ever thrown my way.

Following the transplant I would be in 'confinement' (or quarantine!) to reduce the risk of infection. Children would not be allowed in. We had great confidence in our consultant in Dublin (Dr Conneally) and trusted her advice in all decisions, but leaving to go down for the transplant was by far one of the hardest things I have ever done. Essentially there was no choice, but saying goodbye to the children and not knowing whether I would see them in six weeks, six months or ever again this side of eternity was horrendous. As it turned out I had to do it twice, because the first time I went down the transplant was cancelled due to a slight infection.

For Ruth the distance was hard as well. In New York the hospital was a five minute walk from our apartment. Now it was a three hour drive. She stayed down in Dublin during the week and went back home to the children at the weekend. We both missed them so much. Her parents looked after the children during the week, and my parents looked after me at the weekends!

With hundreds of people and churches praying for us the transplant went very well. I got few serious complications, was discharged to an apartment in Dublin after five weeks, and allowed back up north to be reunited with the children after seven weeks. The reunion for me was amazing and emotional. For them it was as if I'd never been away... 'Hi dad, do you want to play football?'!

BLOWS WHEN I WAS DOWN
During the last two and a half years my emotions have fluctuated considerably. My faith in God has not. There has never been a point when I felt like giving up on God or that somehow I thought he wasn't there. For some, illness is a breaking point in their faith. For me, it wasn't. However, maintaining my relationship with God when I was at my lowest was at times very difficult. Low energy levels, the inability to concentrate, and general inertia ruled out any significant Bible reading for months. I tried reading through the Psalms but at times I couldn't even do that. Ruth would read me people's texts, cards, letters and emails and while at times I found them encouraging, it wasn't always the case. Before I was sick I loved working through books of the Bible and was frustrated by my inability to read any more than a few verses. But it was not guilt. God does not expect us always to be in 'top form' and it is when we are at our lowest that the Spirit intercedes for us (Romans 8:26-27). When I was so unwell, knowing that I could just lie there, still as loved and as firmly held by God as when I was plodding diligently through a Bible commentary, was very comforting.

Having said that, there were several specific instances or 'blows' that seriously diminished my optimism and brought the reality of my situation home. I have already mentioned about initially being told I was 'Philadelphia chromosome positive' – the worst prognostic indicator. After my induction chemotherapy I wasn't discharged from MSK in time for Conor's birthday because my white count hadn't recovered quickly enough (I had thought I would be home well before his birthday). Having set that as a 'goal post' I remember being gutted at the time. The withdrawal of funding from MSK and the consequences of that were hard to adjust to. The readmission with vincristine-induced ileus was particularly difficult to digest. Coming 'home' at Christmas 2007 was also tough. But three other situations stand out as particularly difficult to understand, to accept, and ultimately to deal with.

1. LOSING MY 'IDENTITY'

For ten years I had been a doctor. For most of that I had been a cardiothoracic surgeon, albeit in training. But like Jonah in the Old Testament and so many others I had become defined by what I did. I was proud to be a cardiothoracic surgeon. I had trained hard to get there. But *en route* I had somehow forged an identity for myself without God's word. In so doing I was somehow running further from my true identity because that identity can only come from God. We can all be a good person, a kind person, a faithful person, a churchgoer, a giver, even an elder...and yet still be basing our identity outside of God and his word.

We tell ourselves that the reason I'm a good person is because of my job, I give to charity, I'm involved in church, I have a good marriage, my children have done so well, I spend so much of my time doing things for others, I give so much of my money away. But if that is how we define our identity then when things go wrong, as they ultimately will, when we lose our job, get demoted, struggle in our marriage, lose a loved one, get sick...then despite all the churchgoing, all the Bible reading, all the tithing, all the moral and upright living imaginable, our self-made identity implodes, because we have not based our identity on God and his word.

This became more apparent when I developed leukaemia. Suddenly my work stopped and so somehow did my identity. It didn't hit me so much in New York. I had been a 'Fellow' in the hospital and everyone knew me. But ironically when we returned 'home' to Northern Ireland and began meeting new people I struggled with what to say in response to 'so what do you do?' 'Well I was a cardiothoracic surgeon but I've got leukaemia so now I'm off on sick leave' and so on became very untidy and longwinded.

But as God's word spoke to me, to loosen my grip on the good things God had given me so they didn't become 'God-things', I saw the need to reorientate my priorities so that God was back at the centre of my life, and rediscover that my true identity was as a child of God, not as a cardiothoracic surgeon.

2. RE-ADMISSION TO DUBLIN

I initially did very well following the transplant. I was allowed back home and care became shared again with Belfast (where a close friend who works in the haematology department has been a terrific help over the last two years). But within a couple of months my energy levels dropped significantly. I took to my bed or the sofa as I felt tired most of the day. I didn't have the concentration to read any more and my mood was low and Ruth knew 'something' was different.

All my bloods were 'okay' but Dr Conneally was quick to readmit me on appearance alone and I was subsequently diagnosed with mild 'Graft versus Host disease'. In addition I was referred to see a gastroenterologist, a dietician, a physiotherapist, an occupational therapist and...a psychiatrist, Dr O'Dwyer! I was adamant to Ruth that I certainly did not need a psychiatrist and was even irritated by the suggestion that I did.

I never accepted the diagnosis of depression and still don't. All I felt was extreme fatigue. I never answered her questions with the depth she was looking for. I never had issues to explore. I wasn't being awkward – it was just that I didn't have any hidden hang ups or issues from the past or the present. Despite her understandable frustration with me we developed an excellent relationship. Ultimately when she realised her probing only produced monosyllabic responses from me she would laugh and we would talk about music or rugby. Whatever the problem with my mood, she gave me an exercise programme that began me on a course of recovery that would lead to improvement within days and be the start of a great twelve months of remission, one of the best twelve months of my life, despite the leukaemia. But one that would suddenly and abruptly be changed with the diagnosis of relapse months later...

3. RELAPSE NO 1, NO 2, AND NO 3

I thought I was cured. I knew the statistical likelihood was low but I still thought I was alright. For over a year all the blood tests had been fine.

The genetic markers had also been negative. I felt great. Ruth, having done some haematology, was wisely more reserved.

In April 2009 we were on a weekend in Omagh with about 30 friends from university, including a significant number of offspring! On the first night I was woken from my sleep with excruciating pain in my right thigh. It kept me awake all night but in the morning and with industrial doses of ibuprofen it eased enough to let me join the rest. It was a great weekend but the pain never fully resolved.

Over the next six weeks the pain was controlled with standard painkillers but was gradually increasing in intensity. My bloods were at this stage 'okay' so a family friend who was a radiologist arranged an MRI of my hips (osteonecrosis is a well recognised long term complication of the radiation I had before my transplant). No osteonecrosis was seen. I was sure I was okay!

However, on 17 June we were in clinic in Dublin. We knew by Dr Conneally's face things had changed: 'your bloods aren't good'. My white count was 70. I had relapsed. I was stunned. Apart from leg pain I felt okay. We were due to go on holiday in two weeks. I had even planned to go back to cardiothoracic surgery in August. Ruth and I just looked at each other. We both knew what relapse meant but I think she was less shocked than me.

We elected for outpatient treatment. I knew it wasn't to cure, but just to 'prolong'. The prognosis had now become so grim that the last thing I wanted was to spend weeks in hospital away from the children having aggressive chemotherapy, only to find I hadn't gone into remission at the end of it. Dr Conneally was kind and gentle, explaining that the treatment would come from Belfast rather than Dublin.

The next day we were seen in Belfast where my white count had risen to 90. It was now unclear whether any treatment was going to be effective. Although we are both medical we asked the consultant how things were likely to progress should the treatment be ineffective. During the course of our discussion the consultant's mobile phone went off. It was answered and a brief conversation took place. On returning to our discussion of how I was likely to die it was again interrupted to make a note from the phone call. It was a poor example of breaking bad news.

Two days later we returned; Ruth, Steve (our friend from Cambridge) and me. The duty doctor told us that despite the steroids my white count had more than doubled (to over 180) and a consultant would speak to us shortly. We were ushered into the only available room. When the consultant came in we were left in no uncertainty that this was the end. I would die in the next few days, and no review appointment should be made.

But the immediate clinical prediction turned out to be wrong. The weekend was a blurred 'pre-death wake' thing with many people coming to say what they thought would be their final farewell. But I survived the weekend. Moreover, a blood test on the Sunday showed a dramatic return of the white count to normal!

By this stage, however, I felt miserable; physically, mentally and spiritually. I was tired, and devastated that the leukaemia had returned. I spent the following week in bed. Sometimes asleep, sometimes awake, often in that strange twilight zone between. It was also very hard for Ruth. We both found it hard to compute. Surely I had done my 'suffering' and come through it. Why was I then being allowed to relapse with no prospect of cure? We would have been justified in doing so, and many thought we should, but thankfully we decided not to tell the children just how sick I was, and certainly we didn't say I was about to die. Writing this nearly eight months later I still don't know how we would have handled that, if having told them, I then got better.

We had planned to go for most of July to our favourite place in Donegal – Carrickfin. I felt dreadful but we both thought we should go ahead as planned. We could come back weekly to attend hospital appointments and continue oral medications as if we were at home. We bundled an 'emergency' pack (intravenous fluids, antibiotics, syringes, Venflons and needles, etc), three children and a week's supply of food into the already heavily packed car and headed north and very west!

The year before, after Dr O'Dwyer's exercise plan was set in place, we had spent the month of July in Carrickfin. That month in 2008 transformed me. Having been sofa-bound I arrived and almost immediately began playing sport again with the children. Within days I sledged down the sand dunes and even braced the Donegal Atlantic – a swim not for the faint hearted! Amazingly, for such a remote part of Donegal, Carrickfin is also home to the Donegal airport. With two flights per day Ruth and I flew to our clinic appointments in Dublin! Our caravan had a fabulous view of the sea; however, it was situated in a fully functioning cow field. Not realising my propensity to infection with continuing immunosuppression, the cows showed little concern about where they decided to defaecate! Despite this I avoided all infections, had never felt better, and will always remember July 2008 as a great month and a therapeutic period of recovery.

In July 2009 we weren't in the caravan. We stayed in a wonderful cottage right on the beach with unparallelled views of the Atlantic coastline. But things did not run to the same time-frame and the Donegal air did not seem to be having the same effect, at least not initially. For the first week I continued to stay in bed. I was miserable. I wouldn't go as far as to say I questioned God, but I certainly questioned why I had been 'allowed' to relapse, or having relapsed, why I was still alive but with no strength or energy to be of any use to anyone, especially to Ruth and the children. I occasionally surfaced to take my tablets but basically couldn't be bothered talking to anyone. The children were having a great time but I couldn't even watch them play. Seeing them play just made me sad. I found it heart-wrenching when they asked me to join in, knowing I could barely even get to the beach (a one minute climb down the slope) never mind dig sand castles once I arrived. I didn't think I would see the end of the summer, the children thought I would be there for ever. It was also very hard for Ruth. On the one hand she would play with the children, helping them enjoy their holiday, but on the other she knew that her time with me was now limited.

However, what we didn't know was how limited our time together would be. We went back up to Belfast once a week for blood tests, more chemotherapy and blood or platelet transfusion. Slowly my strength and energy began to improve. It wasn't sudden or dramatic, but it was noticeable and encouraging. My mood improved too. I had not stopped praying and reading but the ability to concentrate on reading and praying grew. I read John Piper's *Seeing and Savouring the Lord Jesus*. I read CJ Maheney's *Cross-centred Life*. Each week the blood tests seemed more stable. In spite of my prognosis I almost felt exhilarated with what God was doing. It appeared the Lord had granted me more time. I remember laughing with Ruth when she said you might even still be here at Christmas – I was beginning to feel well again but I didn't quite have that time-frame in mind. By the end of our month in Donegal I was playing cricket with the children again, I was walking the beach every day, and yes, I even faced the Donegal Atlantic again…only this time with the precaution of a 5mm wetsuit!

August turned out to be a great month. Although fatigue was an issue, I was pretty much back to my old self. A bone marrow biopsy showed I was back in remission…or the Lord's 'permission', haematologically and genetically! In September it was decision time again. A technique called Donor Lymphocyte Infusion could be used to give me some more blood cells from the original donor. These would in theory wipe out the residual leukaemic cells. But it was unproven in acute lymphoblastic leukaemia and had never been shown to improve survival significantly. In addition there was a strong risk of Graft versus Host disease. We prayed about it and decided to go for it. God often works through the normal ways that are in front of us. If it worked, great, if it didn't at least we wouldn't turn round and say 'if only'.

Whether or not it had any effect on things or not we'll never know. But I didn't get Graft versus Host disease and continued to enjoy good health in September and October. I was by now convinced God had worked a miracle in June when I was given days to live. I was convinced it wasn't just to spend more time with my family, although that was for me the number one priority. I felt strong, and more than ever the desire and need to speak to people and persuade them of the power of the gospel was burning inside. I remember receiving an email from a friend in Cambridge who also had terminal cancer. His prayer for his final weeks and months was to fight sin more in his life, rely on Jesus more, and preach Jesus more clearly. I have tried to make those my prayer as well. God had surely raised me up to honour and glorify him, not just enjoy more of the good things he had given me. I started preaching again and meeting people for coffee (but I usually picked them intentionally because they weren't a Christian, or they were a Christian who I could hopefully share my passion with). I recorded a piano CD and got back together with an old band from university. It was like a scene from *The Blues Brothers*. A close friend from the band called: 'the band is getting back together' he said 'and we want you to be in on it!'

We continued to enjoy great family times together but in November I felt a new lump. I still felt well but the genetics had again turned positive. The lump was irradiated without biopsy as the likelihood was

isolated leukaemic recurrence. Relapse was again on the cards.
I received some more chemotherapy and a short course of steroids but life generally continued as normal and we didn't tell many people this had happened. I was disappointed, but spiritually I didn't seem to waver. I had known this was coming and God seemed to give me incredible strength just when I needed it. In some ways it was as if the unexpected relapse in June helped to prepare me, and to some extent Ruth, for the inevitable.

I have always believed God can heal me completely, but I was becoming increasingly aware and even accepting that it appeared he was choosing not to. I continued to preach. Ruth and I continued to live active and busy lives but again we knew the end point was now closer. I remember thinking it was a bit like waiting for a car to come over the horizon. The car represented 'death' and was at some point going to knock me down. Now I could see the car, but just didn't know the speed at which it was travelling.

I did make Christmas...and it was great. The children had a great time, Ruth and I enjoyed it, and Christmas dinner has never tasted so good! But most of December I had colds and coughs. My energy levels were slowly going down and shortly after Christmas the bloods tests showed the leukaemia was back in the peripheral blood. I had formally relapsed again. I still felt okay but all treatment efforts would now be aimed at limiting disease proliferation, or put another way, keeping me alive as long as possible. Again however, we were upset and we were disappointed, but through God's strength alone we didn't crumble. I started to see the car from my analogy not coming to knock me down, but to pick me up. The car wasn't death, it was life. It was now much closer, but I still don't know how fast it is travelling.

I know that you can do all things, and that no purpose of yours can be thwarted...I had heard of you by the hearing of the ear, but now my eye sees you

JOB 42:2,5

In certain parts of the world sheep must once a year go through a decontaminating antiseptic tank in order to prevent them getting certain infections. It does, I'm told, hurt them. It stings, and they certainly try their best to get out of it. The farmer's job is to hold them completely under (often a significant struggle) long enough to ensure they are fully covered and cleaned by the antiseptic. But despite how much he may want to, there is no way the farmer could ever communicate to the sheep what he is doing or why he is doing it: 'It's okay, it's for your good, I'm thinking of you, I'm not just doing this for fun'. The sheep will never understand.

One of the most inevitable things in this life is that if we live long enough, we will suffer. In chapters 1 and 2 of Job we see seemingly arbitrary, absurd and undeserved suffering. But we also see that despite appearance, God is totally sovereign in everything. We see that we can endure our suffering not just because we believe in the sovereignty of a gracious and merciful God but because God 'wrote himself into the play' and underwent the ultimate unjust, undeserved, unmerited human suffering...for us. But suffering is only difficult (intellectually) for the Christian. If you don't believe in God then you do not have to reconcile an omnipotent God with an all-loving God. The unbeliever may wonder why the world is so unfair, but the believer should wonder it one thousand times more.

In the second section we saw that if this book had finished at chapter 2 it would be inauthentic and unreal. It is because Job deals with his suffering long term over many months, and struggles in such a normal human way, that his story can be so helpful to us in our difficulties.

Finally we come to look at Job's suffering from God's perspective. After remaining quiet for so long God finally begins speaking to Job. And we're going to look at chapters 32-42 in three ways: through the pain that heals, the God who speaks, and the servant who worships. As Elihu appeals to Job in 36:2, let me appeal to you: 'Bear with me a little, and I will show you, for I have yet something to say on God's behalf'.

ELIHU: THE PAIN THAT HEALS

We come to chapter 32 of Job. Initially Job was solid. He stood firm with faith in chapters 1 and 2, but as his misery dragged on Job wavered in his confidence that God was for him, and doubted that God was there. But God was trying to speak to Job in and through his pain, not by removing it. Perhaps God wants to speak to you during your suffering because it is only then that you may fully listen. He's not quite ready to lift it, to remove it, to make it all better, because he has more to say *in* your pain rather than *instead* of it.

Historically many commentators class Elihu with the other three friends, just a younger version; an upstart, still cruel, cold, and detached. I do not believe that all of what Elihu says is correct, or at least is correctly applied, but I agree with those who think Elihu actually begins to speak the truth on God's behalf. Elihu was angry (32:2) because he realised the stakes were more than just the suffering of one man. As the barrage of the friends' attacks dies away, Elihu's words are not just theological rhetoric, but include much that Job will find hard, yet useful to listen to. Here are three reasons why.

First, Elihu's words are not introduced as a continuation or repetition of what the friends have said. Remember, the three friends basically told Job he was suffering because he had sinned. The guilty suffer, and the innocent do okay. But (32:3): 'He [Elihu] burned with anger also at Job's three friends because they had found no answer, although they had declared Job to be in the wrong'. Elihu disagrees with both sides. He has no intention of picking up where Eliphaz, Bildad and Zophar left off their arguments: 'I will not answer him with your speeches' (32:14).

Secondly, the last 30 chapters have been taken up with Job arguing back at his friends, dismantling their argument, and overturning their reasoning. But this time Job doesn't try to argue with Elihu, even though he is given the chance to do so in 33:32: 'If you have any words, answer me; speak, for I desire to justify you. If not, listen to me; be silent, and I will teach you wisdom.' It's not that Elihu gives Job an easy time. He doesn't say 'don't worry Job mate, you're alright'. He does rebuke Job: 'Job speaks without knowledge; his words are without insight. Would that Job were tried to the end, because he answers like wicked men. For he adds rebellion to his sin; he claps his hands among us and multiplies his words against God' (34:35-37). So there must be something different in what Elihu says.

Thirdly, God doesn't rebuke Elihu as he does the other three friends at the end of chapter 42.

For the first time, Elihu is suggesting that God may actually be using Job's suffering to change him. He is suggesting that his suffering is for a purpose. Elihu slowly introduces us to a theology of what John Piper calls 'corrective suffering'. I am aware just how sensitive this may be for some and how hard this may be to appreciate, but I am compelled to say what I believe the Bible is teaching. Elihu thinks Job has been wrong in some of what he's said:

Surely you have spoken in my ears, and I have heard the sound of your words. You say, 'I am pure, without transgression; I am clean, and there is no iniquity in me. Behold, he finds occasions against me, he counts me as his enemy, he puts my feet in the stocks and watches all my paths.' Behold, in this you are not right (33:8-12).

Job's suffering leads him to say things that are too optimistic of himself, and too disrespectful of God; Job is righteous (chapter 1) but he is still a sinner. Job still had the remnant of pride and self-reliance, but it only became apparent when he was really shaken, pushed to the edge, when the pressure was on.

We don't really get to know someone when everything is going well. It's only when things get tough, when the wheels fall off, that we see people's true colours shining through. I'm not a fan of television's *I'm a Celebrity; Get Me Out Of Here* but it can highlight how people react or don't react when they're under pressure, when the make-up, the mascara and the mirror are removed and the real them is exposed. As a medical student, around a coffee and scones, I could argue my point of view with the best of them. But in the exam situation, when, as one examiner told me, 'the true depths of my surgical knowledge would be exposed' it was a very different story. Pressure exposes the real us, and pain even more so. This idea causes CS Lewis to write: 'Pain insists upon being attended to. God whispers to us in our pleasures, speaks in our conscience, but shouts in our pains.'[15]

I'm not detracting from Job's initial faith. What an amazing man of faith. God had in fact initially used Job's faith, during his suffering, to demonstrate to Satan himself and to others that God's glory was more important than anything else to Job. But as his suffering went on a new purpose of God was at hand; to purge out of Job the remnant of pride and the sediment of self-centredness that still lay at the bottom of Job's life.

Pain and suffering in and of themselves are never good – they are only bad or perhaps sometimes neutral. They are part of the Fall. They won't be part of heaven. So what can then be good and of long term benefit is not the pain and suffering *per se*, but how we deal with them.

Do you know how natural pearls are created? It all starts with a tiny worm that bores through the oyster in the sea. Water then carries specks of sand into the oyster which irritate and even hurt the oyster. The pain is negative and of no benefit until the oyster begins to deal with it by excreting a substance to cover the sand. This process is repeated and repeated until an embryonic pearl begins to grow and grow. And so the initial pain leads to something of immense beauty and worth.

There are perhaps then two purposes to be fulfilled in Job's suffering. The first is to glorify God's name, as demonstrated in chapters 1 and 2. But the second is to sanctify Job's life. In his book *Dying, the greatest adventure of my life* James Casson writes: 'at one time I became bitter against God because I felt like he was looking on rather like a torture-supervisor, quietly authorising more and more distressing experiences to see how soon, I, the prisoner would crack. The rack was slowly tightening, the thumbscrew remorselessly turned.'[16] But the pain God permits is not the pain of a torturer's whip but that of a surgeon's scalpel.

---

15. CS Lewis. *The Problem of Pain*. (First published 1940.) London: Fount, 1998. p74
16. James Casson. *Dying - the greatest adventure of my life*. CMF, 1999. p22

Surgery is cruel if performed by a novice, but it can be life saving if performed by an expert, although it may still be painful. Similarly, suffering can be seen as reckless and cruel, absurd and unmerited when we try and understand it from a human perspective, as a novice in the things of God. But when we see it from God's perspective, then we can see spiritual transformation that heals and saves.

When you get your hernia repaired, or your gallbladder removed, or your varicose veins taken out, in the UK you can more or less guarantee the surgeon you get will know what he's doing (I accept the odd story in the paper may suggest otherwise!) But when God uses pain as a tool to change our life, and to make us more Christ-like, then the Bible can completely guarantee us that God completely knows what he is doing, all of the time. Even though it can hurt so badly at times, and even though we don't see why at times. So rather than pray for the weight to be lifted from our shoulders, sometimes we should just pray for stronger shoulders. This experience of suffering does not seek a supernatural release from distress (although that can happen) but it seeks a supernatural release *through* and *in* the distress. The perspective we must attain is to understand what God's ultimate plan for us is, even in this life. As John Stott approaches the 'end of his pilgrimage on earth' he comments that God's purpose for his people is to make us become like Christ: 'Christ-likeness is the will of God for the people of God.' [17]

Job is discovering a pain that heals. But ultimately it is only in Jesus that we discover a pain that heals completely. Job endured suffering for his own good. Jesus endured a pain in order that others might be healed – namely you and me. Isaiah 53: 4-5: 'Surely he has borne *our* griefs and carried *our* sorrows; yet we esteemed him stricken, smitten by God, and afflicted. But he was wounded for *our* transgressions; he was crushed for *our* iniquities; upon him was the chastisement that brought *us* peace, and with his stripes *we* are healed.' (Emphasis added.) It is only by the suffering of Jesus, not by our suffering, that our pain is ever fully healed.

According to Elihu the suffering of the righteous, the blameless (as Job is described in chapter 1) is a token of God's love and a refinement of their righteousness: 'For God speaks in one way, and in two, though man does not perceive it...that he may turn man aside from his deed and conceal pride from a man' (33:14,17). Job's three friends were wrong, but Job has

17. Roger Steer. *Inside Story. The life of John Stott*. IVP, 2009. p271

also been wrong. Elihu says suffering is not a proof of sin, but neither is it a proof of God's arbitrariness or randomness.

Psalm 119:71: 'It is good for me that I was afflicted, that I might learn your statutes'. God opens an ear *through* affliction. Elihu's new slant, that the first three friends failed to grasp, is that the suffering of the righteous is not the fire of destruction but the fire that refines their goodness, not punitive but corrective. John Piper writes 'No pain is too great to endure in this life if it helps us to submit and trust more fully and remove all the pride'. The apostle Paul writes to the church in Rome that our sufferings are not even worth comparing with the glory that will be revealed in us (Romans 8:18).

Again I do not presume to know your circumstances, but I wonder: is there any way in which God is speaking to you *in* your pain? Healing you *in* your suffering? Refining you *through* your distress? Consider the words of CS Lewis and ask yourself: is God using your tragedy to be his 'megaphone'?

THE LORD: A GOD WHO SPEAKS

Job has had a tough time. He had now been lying in unrelieved misery for months. Aside from his dreadful skin condition he had endured the horrific loss of seven dead sons and three dead daughters. All his wealth was gone. His wife regarded him as repulsive, his brothers as loathsome, and even the little children despised him.

God had permitted Satan enough 'slack on his leash' to inflict this pain, but Job's pain seems to have been made worse by his faith, not better. For 36 chapters Job thinks the God he once knew has remained totally silent. If he was an atheist he would put it all down to chance, or memes, or atoms, or physics.

But because he has been trying to hold on to God he can't bear to think God is out there but just ignoring him. Someone said 'it is better to have loved and lost, than never to have loved at all'…but I don't think Job would agree with that right now.

But now God does finally speak. We may wonder why God didn't speak earlier. One reason could be to show us he will not be forced into quick responses, forced into our time frame. Our God is not an emailing God. He doesn't reply to our texts as soon as the beep goes. He doesn't post comments on Facebook or Twitter, but rather he replies precisely when he means to. He acts in his time, and in his way. You may be waiting to hear God's voice. You may be wondering if he hears your cries and your prayers, if he feels your pain, if he will respond. The answer is yes, yes, yes...he does and he will, but he does so in his time, not ours.

Chapter 38 starts brilliantly:

Then the Lord answered Job out of the whirlwind and said: 'Who is this that darkens counsel by words without knowledge? Dress for action like a man; I will question you, and you make it known to me.' (38:1-3)

I don't know if you watch *The Apprentice*, but if you do you might recall the nervous candidates as they face Sir Alan in the boardroom...especially if they think they're about to get fired. Sir Alan, in his inimitable arrogance, doesn't ever lower himself to allow them even to suggest he may be wrong, that his opinion may somehow be inaccurate. 'Who are you to question my authority, my expertise, and my empire?'

But when we consider the things of the Almighty Creator God, who on earth would dare to question his judgment? We often perceive God as gentle and kind, almost like a friendly grandfather. But here, as echoed in Nahum 1:3, sometimes 'His way is in whirlwind and storm, and the clouds are the dust of his feet'.

But let us first note some things about what God does *not* say which we might have expected him to. He doesn't take Job by the hand and lead him to all the answers. He doesn't directly answer all the 'why?' questions of Job. He doesn't apologise for not getting back to Job sooner. He doesn't tell Job about the deal with Satan and he doesn't sympathise with Job about how immense his suffering has been. Rather he expects Job (and us) to accept not knowing the answers to all our questions and just to bow before him as the Creator and Sovereign God.

We must constantly remind ourselves that his ways are not our ways and his thoughts are not our thoughts (Isaiah 55:8). He is God and we are not. He isn't required to explain himself to us. This is the perspective we need to recover. So often we have that image of God as a big buddy for fun and fellowship, like a genie or a fairy godmother. We thank him for his intimacy but forget he is also the sovereign Almighty God.

Instead of answering Job's burning questions, God takes him on a whistle-stop tour of creation:

Where were you when I laid the foundation of the earth? Tell me, if you have understanding. Who determined its measurements – surely you know! Or who stretched the line upon it? On what were its bases sunk, or who laid its cornerstone, when the morning stars sang together and all the sons of God shouted for joy? Or who shut in the sea with doors when it burst out from the womb, when I made clouds its garment and thick darkness its swaddling band, and prescribed limits for it and set bars and doors, and said, 'Thus far shall you come, and no farther, and here shall your proud waves be stayed'? (38:4-11)

God amazes Job by the intricacy and complexity of it all, and impresses on him that there is a divine order and pattern. God really does have the whole world in his hands. Job doesn't. He never has, he never will; and neither do we nor will we. Job is utterly impotent and surrounded by mystery, by things he doesn't understand and over which he has no control. We are too, even with so many scientific discoveries. God is much less impressed by our science than we are.

In chapter 39 God reinforces to Job that every time something happens, God is there. I know and created all things. Do you know anything about any of the ten billion things going on in the world right now...and yet knowing none of these things what can you presume to tell me about how to run the world? I have a handle on everything and yet you will suggest to me what is wise and what is unwise!

God is not trying to rub Job's nose in it but is helping Job to see things from the heavenly perspective – we are small, ignorant and impotent when compared with God. Yet God still loves Job so much that he wants him ultimately to be refined, to be saved, and to be restored. God is God and we are not.

But there *is* one person who can answer all of God's questions to Job in chapter 39 with a definitive yes...and that person is Jesus Christ. Jesus alone can say to God 'when you laid the earth's foundation I was there too. When you marked off its dimensions I was there. When you stretched a measuring line across it I was there. While the morning stars sang together and all the angels shouted for joy I was there and I was singing too.' But because God loves us, Jesus had to come down. He wrote himself into the play so that while we will never have God's wisdom this side of eternity we can have a person. God gave us himself in the form of his son, Jesus, to hold on to as we face our struggles and our suffering. We have a person who says to us that, whatever we're going through, he has been through it before us and is now there to hold us and lead us. When we realise that, as Job ultimately did, then we will become a servant who worships.

JOB: THE SERVANT WHO WORSHIPS

In chapter 40 God pauses to allow Job to respond and he does: 'Then Job answered the Lord and said: "Behold, I am of small account; what shall I answer you? I lay my hand on my mouth. I have spoken once, and I will not answer; twice, but I will proceed no further."' (40:3-5). Job is a finite creature who knows nothing of 99.999999999% of what's going on and has no right to question God. Job did overstep the mark a bit and now he needs to be silent. 33:31,33: 'Pay attention, O Job, listen to me; be silent, and I will speak...If not, listen to me; be silent, and I will teach you wisdom.' The Bible repeats that message – 'Be still and know that I am God' (Psalm 46:10). There is so much we don't know and will never know, and wouldn't understand even if we did know, that there are times when we must just be silent before our creator. Today the media may say that's not very 'politically correct' – with freedom of information we should know why everything that happens to us is happening to us. But silence before God, our Lord, our sovereign deity, is often exactly what is required – how long do we spend silently before God each day, each week?

Then silence is broken and Job does speak again to God, only this time his tone is humble and repentant. 42:2-3: 'I know that you can do all things, and that no purpose of yours can be thwarted. "Who is this that hides counsel without knowledge?" Therefore I have uttered what I did not understand, things too wonderful for me, which I did not know.'

Job has admitted he doesn't understand the cosmos. God brings Job to submission by saying 'There is so much going on of which you are totally ignorant. Therefore you have no right, warrant or sense in admonishing, counselling or advising me how to run the world. When I exert my sovereign power I don't do it whimsically, I do it deliberately. I am a loving physician and my pain is a pain that ultimately heals and restores.' Job finally submits to the absolute sovereignty of God. No one can thwart

God's purposes; there is knowledge and wisdom so far beyond his ability to comprehend, and he has been foolish even to question it. God's goodness is not irrational, capricious or arbitrary and Job is to submit to, rather than to condemn, his God. Job's experience taught him so much more than his friends' theology ever would. 42:5: 'I had heard of you by the hearing of the ear, but now my eye sees you'. Five seconds of seeing, of experiencing, is worth more than five days in the study. You can read all you want about religion and suffering, you can even go to church all you want, but until you experience God's goodness and submit to his sovereignty you will never be changed.

Until God came and addressed himself to Job it was all just theory. Job is now a changed and a broken man, but a servant ready for God to use. God is after us all having a brokenhearted childlike heart of faith - whatever it takes and whatever it costs, and that may include suffering, to get us to a place where we can be used by him. That's where he now has Job, with a brokenhearted childlike faith, not a pious, proud, theoretical religion.

CONCLUSION

Finally all that Job had lost was given back to him (42:10). All that we once had may not be returned to us in this life. The Bible gives us no assurance of that. But be assured there will be glory for those who have suffered with Christ, even if death ends the suffering in this life in order that we partake in the ultimate glory.

Though our outer self is wasting away, our inner self is being renewed day by day. For this light momentary affliction is preparing for us an eternal weight of glory beyond all comparison, as we look not to the things that are seen but to the things that are unseen. For the things that are seen are transient, [the sickness, the death, the pain, the suffering] *but the things that are unseen are eternal.* (2 Corinthians 4:16-18)

The seeking we need to adopt is not for the answers to our philosophical questions, but rather to seek God himself. That is where Job is directing us. There is no fully satisfying intellectual answer to Job's pain, but there is grace, because suffering is not a problem requiring a solution but a mystery requiring a presence. That presence is a crucified, abandoned Christ, who suffered with us and for us. The living God is not to be debated, questioned and qualified, but to be encountered on a cross, worshipped and adored.

REFLECTIONS

The only thing to do with good advice is pass it on

OSCAR WILDE

When I first had contact with CMF about the possibility that the sermons I had written up might be published, I was asked to flesh out the narrative of my personal journey, and to suggest some advice both for those who are patients and for their health professionals and carers.

GIVING AND RECEIVING ADVICE

I have always been slightly cautious of people who love to give advice, and particularly so of those who have 'been there, seen it, done it'. Some people inundated us and advised us of their personal technique or way of getting through. Much as they meant well, and I hope to cause no offence by this, everyone is different and that includes the ways we respond to and cope with suffering and sickness.

I think there are invaluable lessons to learn from other people, particularly those who can direct us to God's word, rather than to their specific recipe or 'get well manual'. Having said that, I know many who have benefitted significantly from cancer patient networks and who enjoy sharing their story with people who have been through similar problems. So I am completely supportive of the concept.

However, personally I rarely found chatting to other cancer patients helpful, and often very unhelpful. That is with the exception of two leukaemia patients I now know well. The problem with sharing my story and what we have learned from it is how we put our 'wisdom' across to individuals. My healing or lack of healing bears no relation to what will happen to someone else - except to acknowledge we have a great God who has the power to heal *should he choose to do so*. I can say with ease that I learned far more from Steve Midgley, who has never had cancer, from his gentle guiding to God's word (and his silence) than I did from all the many cancer patients I met who added their wisdom to our situation. I love them and respect them all for the way they have coped and are coping with their disease, but I firmly believe it is God's word that is the best source of practical advice.

UNHELPFUL ADVICE

There were two things I found most difficult during my illness, and again I mean no harm - things were always well meant and said with the best intentions. I mention them at all to highlight that things were often said because of a lack of medical understanding of the specific disease process.

The first concerns people who talked about all cancers as if they were the same: 'John had cancer too and he did fine...you should be okay'. Anyone reading this should be aware that many cancers are very different with huge variation in outcome. Someone with end-stage liver cancer cannot be compared to someone with early-stage testicular cancer.

Secondly, and I may be at odds with many people here, but I do not believe the 'power of positive thinking' changes the outcome of a particular cancer. I think it's good and important. It may help someone's mood and it may make someone more optimistic. It may enable them to go out and live a more normal life. However, people persistently (and again with the best intentions) telling you to 'stay positive' become increasingly frustrating. God heals, he *can* work miracles, people defy the odds, but generally speaking medical statistics exist because across a population that is usually what happens when a group of people have the same disease. It's not 'unchristian' or demonstrating a lack of faith to believe the statistics. If the statistics say you're going to die it is appropriate to plan for your death even with the belief that God still has power to heal completely - that is realism, not unfaithful pessimism. God can heal at any stage but death is the 'final enemy' that we all must face at some time.

MAINTAINING DEVOTIONAL LIFE

There were times in my treatment when I could barely think, let alone pray or read. But when I could I found short readings easier. There were other days when I didn't read any of God's word and barely prayed more than a few words. But when I did, against all my natural instincts I learned to set my quiet time targets very low. Rather than hoping to read the whole of Ezekiel in one sitting and then being disappointed when I didn't get past chapter one, I would only plan to read a few verses at a time (and not of Ezekiel!). I don't always use Bible reading notes but I relied on them heavily in hospital.

A short section of the Bible is also easier to mull over and think about during the day. In fact, repeating the same section again and again wasn't boring, but I found it helpful as God's Spirit continued to illuminate and explain. In Psalm 1 when it speaks about the righteous man meditating 'day and night' the idea is of repeating scripture to yourself over and over again, almost mumbling it under your breath. Work it in until it becomes a part of you. When you're sick you generally can't go far, so what better way to spend those otherwise miserable and often lonely hours than thinking about God's word, over and over again.

Ruth never stopped going to church and taking the children with her. For some the music in church can be too emotional when under stress but as Ruth used to say, if she stopped going, when do you restart? In addition, not only can church be a good distraction (particularly for the spouse), but being taught God's word must remain a lifeline, even when we don't always want to hear what God has to say.

I found it was hugely helpful letting others read the Bible to me and pray with me and for me. Open wards limit this to some extent but don't stop it. In particular, when I couldn't eat or drink, Steve shared his 'quiet time' with me and I was greatly encouraged. I was able to attend the weekly prayer meeting held by my closest friends before I went for my transplant. They arranged it in my house and it was great. Rather than vague platitudes and general encouragement, I found friends and family who had an intentional or specific 'word' for me in the particular situation we were in helpful, because that situation changes. I remember one close friend sharing with me from I Kings 19 about Elijah when he felt he couldn't keep going. While he was sleeping an angel came, and didn't remove him from the place but rather provided him with a meal. That meal was just enough to allow Elijah to continue. Again I found this so relevant to where I was at; it had been specifically thought about by my friend.

Reading books is not really an option when things are at their worst. But as recovery slowly took place I found simple and short books useful regardless of what I might have read prior to becoming unwell.

Finally I listened to a lot of music. iPods, MP3 players etc make this so easy and if one is not available, borrow, beg and plead for one. Not that I am pious, but while I was very unwell I only ever listened to sacred music. At times it was very emotional as I listened through my favourite worship songs, but alone in my room at bedtime I actually found it very comforting. Some close friends in Cambridge sent me some music they knew I would love. It was kind. It was intentional. It was thoughtful. As I got better I started to listen to other music and I realised the chemo hadn't completely wiped out my love for jazz and blues!

WANTING TO BE A DOCTOR BUT WILLING TO BE A PATIENT
I suppose this section is mainly of interest to medical staff but I hope everyone can derive some benefit from it...

My status had changed overnight. I was no longer the 'Thoracic Fellow', but the guy with leukaemia in room 12B. But as a patient in 12B, in Belfast and ultimately in Dublin I learned more about some aspects of patient care than I learned in 15 years of medical education. It would take another book to convey half of what I learned but I want to focus on three aspects.

1. NEVER FORGET A PATIENT'S DIGNITY
I discovered that being a patient can be a very humbling and at times a humiliating experience. I remember my first outpatient clinic visit after I had been discharged to the flat in New York. I walked the five minutes to the hospital but by the time I got to clinic I was so tired I had to lie down on the floor in the middle of the waiting area. I was so embarrassed, but at the same time too exhausted to care. The clinic nurse came and asked if I was okay and in that ridiculous Irish mannerism of not wanting to cause anyone any trouble I replied (flat out on the ground in the middle of a busy clinic): 'Yeah, I'm fine thanks!'

For all my treatment in New York and Dublin I was in a side room. When receiving some maintenance chemo in Belfast I was mainly in an open ward. I found this more difficult than I would have thought. When visitors came I felt you couldn't hold a normal conversation because everyone in the ward could hear. There was certainly no possibility of private discussions. Curtains are not soundproof. In return you could also hear everything from the other patients. Chatting with visiting relatives is one thing, but hearing everything from vomiting to fruity coughing to unending flatulence does not make your stay any more enjoyable. One particularly amusing incident was that when I tried turning the TV on at my bed space, the remote somehow managed to change channels on the TV across the ward. The patient and his relatives were in the middle of watching a tense football match, so suddenly being switched to the latest soap did not impress. I closed my eyes hoping they wouldn't figure out what had happened!

The NHS certainly can't afford single rooms across the board, and some patients enjoy the company an open ward provides. But as a doctor I was unaware of the extent of the infringement on personal dignity that the open ward causes for some patients. Things became particularly embarrassing when urine samples were needed. The bottle, full or empty, would just lie at the side of your bed. For close friends it was a source of amusement but for less close visitors I found it highly embarrassing.

I realised early that even simple things, like going for a chest X-ray, are major outings for a sick patient. The wheelchair trip through hospital is cold and uncomfortable. But as a Fellow who had worked in the hospital I also found the many X-ray trips embarrassing. Perhaps they shouldn't have been, but many staff knew me. Some acknowledged it and would speak to me, others didn't. From swaggering around the hospital calling the shots I was suddenly in a gown, in a wheelchair, and looking very uncomfortable.

2. PATIENTS HANG ON TO EVERY WORD THE DOCTOR SAYS
In some respects I adapted to the patient role very easily. I didn't know much about leukaemia before my diagnosis but I surprised myself by not wanting to find out much about it after my diagnosis either. Ruth had worked in haematology and therefore knew a lot already. I usually thrived on medical *minutiae* but really didn't care much about the details of 'my' leukaemia. This changed over the years but at the start, apart from the survival statistics, I otherwise showed little interest.

However, the problem with choosing not to know the details is that you then rely on everything the staff tell you. You hang on their every word and their every comment, opinion or advice. In addition, when the doctor drops a casual comment at the end about an investigation or a result, your day then becomes focused on waiting for that investigation or result. As a doctor I don't remember how many times I would have told patients casually we would get a chest X-ray or a scan. For me the day continued as normal. I now realise that for the patient it would be a day waiting and thinking about nothing else but that scan. Medical staff must be aware how much patients cling to what they say, for good and for bad.

3. DOCTORS SHOULD BE CAREFUL BEFORE DISMISSING PATIENTS' AND RELATIVES' CONCERNS

For me this was exemplified when Ruth shared her concerns about me with one member of staff. Ruth had seen me every day for weeks and was concerned something was wrong, that I had gone significantly downhill. In the five minute consultation Ruth was advised to stop being a doctor and just go home to be a good wife. Within days I was readmitted to a different hospital with Graft versus Host disease! I remember as a houseman a wise professor telling me to listen to the patient – they're usually right!

REGRETS

Frank Sinatra sang: 'I've had a few, but then again, too few to mention'. I think Christians have some sort of innate difficulty in mentioning the word 'regret'. It seems to infer some lack of wisdom or conjure up images of backsliding and failure. But to use that classic new educational euphemism, we all have things that we would have done 'differently'.

I don't know if I went back to surgery whether I would be a better doctor or not. But I like to think that I would definitely be a different one. Compassion and concern for the patient would be much more of a priority than they were before my illness. Attending to patients' questions and concerns, however seemingly trivial or irrelevant, would be much more important. Ward rounds would be slower to allow patients time to ask questions rather than feel like someone on a fast moving conveyor belt. I would try to confirm timing for scans and tests rather than let the patient hang on waiting indefinitely. Similarly I would try to get results to the patient as soon as I knew them. At least this would all be so in an idealistic return to work. Whether I would actually just slip back into the NHS production line I don't know.

Looking back now, with the increased passion I have for the gospel, I am disappointed at so many missed opportunities to share Jesus. Many people are put off by 'church' and 'religion', but I find few who are genuinely put off by Jesus – the real Jesus, the Jesus who helps the poor and the homeless and the unloved, and who ultimately showed his own love for us by being brutally murdered on a cross. I love apologetics and arguing a philosophical defence of the gospel, but it is always Jesus *the person* who changes people's lives, not philosophical debate. Did I spend too much time trying to be clever and not enough time just talking 'Jesus'? I don't know.

I also spent years *talking* about leaving medicine to go into full-time Bible teaching ministry. I always believed at some stage I would, but somehow I never did it. Given the opportunity again, would I leave medicine sooner? I don't know. Christianity needs Bible teachers. It needs good ones and faithful ones. But what we do, wherever we do it, is still Christian ministry. What matters is how we do it. I would certainly use my opportunities in medicine more wisely. I would make my witness more obvious and vocal. Christians must integrate into society to share God's word, rather than become isolated. God wants people in all professions to be witnesses for him, but we must *be* witnesses when we're there, not keep it hidden until Sundays. There is a huge mission field wherever we are.

Finally, if I could do it again, knowing what I've learned over the past couple of years, I would work harder not to let the 'good-things' God has given become 'God-things'. I would definitely do my finances differently, and I hope in a more Christ-like way. I think materialism and consumerism are some of the biggest challenges for authentic Christian living in the western world. I say so because prior to New York, I was up there (or down there) with the best of them. I did my Christianity inside a huge comfort blanket of houses and cars and all things nice. I tithed my tenth, and even more sometimes, but it never really dented my cosy cocoon. Authentic Christian living, Christ-like living requires a huge adjustment of the way we spend our money, our time, and how we juggle our priorities. I often got it wrong, and so yes, I would do some things very differently.

CLOSING THOUGHTS

It all depends how clear our view is of eternity...once this world is seen as a time of preparation, a transit flight, a train journey, then, when I am prepared and God's purpose has been achieved, what is wrong with being shown a short-cut to the summit?

JAMES CASSON [18]

I recently received an email from a friend in Cambridge. He suggests that all of us have a certain frustration from being confined within time. We cannot hold on to time...but our frustration with time suggests that perhaps we are not meant to be confined by it. CS Lewis writes: 'We are so little reconciled to time that we are even astonished at it. 'How he's grown!' we exclaim, 'How time flies!' It's as strange as if a fish were repeatedly surprised at the wetness of water. And that would be strange indeed; unless of course, the fish were destined to become, one day, a land animal.' [19]

Our frustration with time is a reminder that we were not made for time, but for eternity. We are all meant to become (in CS Lewis' image) land animals – to emerge out of time into a greater dimension...but that is only possible because of the resurrection. It is the resurrection that gives us the courage not to fear time, or tomorrow, or whatever may happen to us in this world. Even before it happened, it was the resurrection that gave Job a hope beyond the here and now and into eternity. It was the

18. James Casson. *Dying - the greatest adventure of my life*. CMF, 1999. p32
19. CS Lewis. *Reflections on the Psalms*. Harcourt, Brace, 1958. Chapter 12 'Second Meanings'

resurrection that changed the disciples from deserting cowards into men and women of faith, conviction and courage, and it is the resurrection that can change us and our suffering into something more glorious than we will ever imagine.

In the darkest night of the soul, Christians have something to hold on to that Job never knew – we know a crucified Christ, and we also know a risen Christ. The children of God, those who trust God, who are covered by Jesus' blood, who are being sanctified by his Spirit, still also suffer, but our suffering is overseen by the loving hand of our perfect physician so that our faith might be refined, our holiness might be enlarged, and our God might be glorified.

Let the resurrected Christ lift you up, call you by name, and not only convince your mind and warm your heart but also show you that through himself he now offers a radically new relationship, with cosmic possibilities of intimacy beyond even that which Job could understand. In your daily clinging to God, trust completely in God's sovereignty and pray that God would give you a heart of submission and belief in and through your sufferings.

Believe everything this sovereign God does is for your good and pray that you would see and hear and learn, as Job did, in and through your sufferings. Remember that the purposes of God in the child of suffering are compassionate and merciful. Submit to him, cling to him, give your all to him. And you will one day be restored to more than you could ever possibly imagine.

As an example of suffering and patience...we consider those blessed who remained steadfast. You have heard of the steadfastness of Job, and you have seen the purpose of the Lord, how the Lord is compassionate and merciful

JAMES 5:10-11

I know that my Redeemer lives, and at the last he will stand upon the earth. And after my skin has been thus destroyed, yet in my flesh I shall see God, whom I shall see for myself, and my eyes shall behold, and not another. My heart faints within me!

JOB 19:25-27